We A̶ Saved
TOGETHER

"Colin Miller masterfully paints a portrait of a Church that reveals the loving heart of the artisan who created us all. What could be more attractive? His stories help us to 'see the Gospel' while honoring the legacy of Dorothy Day and Peter Maurin. I'm confident that the founders of the Catholic Worker would delight in this account of the lessons learned from a life lived in community with the 'least' of Christ's brothers and sisters. This book is magnificent—challenging but filled with hope."

Most Rev. Bernard A. Hebda
Archbishop of Saint Paul and Minneapolis

"In this book, Miller spotlights the great problems of loneliness and meaninglessness prevalent in our world today. He beckons us to rediscover the work and vision of Dorothy Day and Peter Maurin who understood the Catholic faith is primarily an adventure, beginning in friendship and culminating in personal sanctity and true worship. Remaining deeply rooted in each other's lives provides a space where Christ can transform the world, one heart at a time."

Colleen Hutt
Director of vision and outreach for Well-Read Mom

"I feel compelled to warn you: this is not a book that can be read casually. If you're curious about Dorothy Day or vaguely interested in 'the poor' as a concept, you might want to keep your distance. Miller has not given us a memoir that leaves the reader vaguely impressed and ready to return to life as it was. No, this book is an examination of conscience, an invitation not merely to evaluate our tithing but to reconsider every element of our lives: the work we do, the food we eat, the places we live. We who seek to follow Jesus can't live ordinary lives of big-box stores and travel soccer with a visit to church most Sundays. No, the Gospel has to change us, to transform us so radically that no part of our lives is untouched. This is a dangerous book, which is just why I hope you read it."

Meg Hunter-Kilmer
Author of *Pray for Us*

"Writing with a wisdom honed by the Gospel's demand to be in community with the poor, Miller reminds his readers that Dorothy Day and Peter Maurin are forgotten at our peril. With a storyteller's gift, Miller introduces us to the world of the Catholic Worker."

Stanley Hauerwas
Author of *A Community of Character: Toward a Constructive Christian Social Ethic*

We Are Only Saved TOGETHER

Living the Revolutionary Vision of DOROTHY DAY and the Catholic Worker Movement

COLIN MILLER

AVE MARIA PRESS AVE Notre Dame, Indiana

Nihil Obstat: Reverend Monsignor Michael Heintz, PhD
               Censor Librorum
Imprimatur: Most Reverend Kevin C. Rhoades
               Bishop of Fort Wayne–South Bend
               Given at Fort Wayne, Indiana, on April 10, 2024

The *Nihil Obstat* and *Imprimatur* are official declarations that a book or pamphlet is free of doctrinal or moral error. No implication is contained therein that those who have granted the *Nihil Obstat* or *Imprimatur* agree with its contents, opinions, or statements expressed.

Foreword © 2024 by Seth Haines.

Founded in 1865, Ave Maria Press is a ministry of the United States Province of Holy Cross.

www.avemariapress.com

Paperback: ISBN-13: 978-1-64680-306-4

E-book: ISBN-13: 978-1-64680-307-1

Cover image of Dorothy Day © Julie Lonneman, used courtesy of trinitystores.com. Image of Peter Maurin © Jim Forest.

Cover design by K.H. Bonelli.

Text design by Samantha Watson.

Printed and bound in the United States of America.

Library of Congress Cataloging-in-Publication Data is available.

CONTENTS

FOREWORD

Colin Miller wrote this book over the coals of a smoldering revolution. Advancements in artificial intelligence promise economic prosperity, and the proponents of this technology see the coming of a new Industrial Revolution. It will be bigger than the birth of the internet, they claim, and will allow us to cure diseases, simplify production, and produce more wealth. It'll lead to abundance. Maybe it will break the chains of human poverty once and for all. The promises of technology—aren't they grandiose?

The pundits, prognosticators, and futurists might be right, but have we truly reckoned with the dehumanizing byproducts of previous industrial revolutions? The divides between rich and poor deepened. The *haves* self-selected into gated communities and suburbs, leaving the *have-nots* isolated and alone. Industrial blight marred the living conditions of those on the margins. In the pursuit of wealth, the poor were forgotten.

In the 1930s, Dorothy Day and Peter Maurin saw the effects of industrialization with clear eyes, and in response, they started the Catholic Worker movement. It was a movement born of a particular age, but it wasn't a movement limited to that age. Colin Miller proves that simple fact in this book, which chronicles his transformation from an everyday Catholic to one of the founding members of a Catholic Worker house. As I read Miller's work and considered the unintended consequences of our modern industrial revolution, I couldn't help but think that his experience provides the antidote to what's poisoning us in this present age.

What is the poison?

The disembodied artificiality that isolates us from each other, particularly those who do not share our social or economic status.

What is that remedy?

True, historically-rooted, non-gentrified, unsegregated, open-handed, open-hearted, flesh-and-blood, Eucharist-shaped Christian community.

In these pages, Miller makes real art. It's not the art you'd hang on your wall or the kind that finds its way into obscure poetry anthologies. Here, Miller shares the art of *humaning together*. It's a deep sacramental art, one that answers our modern conundrum: *How can we be saved from the traps of an increasingly artificial world?*

Through these pages, Miller shows how his interactions with people who were homeless and impoverished moved from transactional to personal to true friendship. Through his eyes, you'll see what's possible when people cross economic barriers and live, work, and till the ground together. Ultimately, you'll see how one group of committed friends made a series of decisions that led to something like salvation.

We live in a politically polarized world, one in which we try to sort people into easy buckets. And as you read this foreword, perhaps you're tempted to throw Miller into the *wild-haired socialist* bucket. Resist that urge. The words of this book are not political, or at least they're no more political than the words of Christ himself. Still, Miller has a lot to say about what ails our current society, and more particularly, what ails the modern Church. He points to our individualism and our failure to live out the Gospel in community, but he doesn't do it with a heavy hand. Instead, through his experience and study, he points us back to the history and tradition of the Church. He reminds us of St. Thérèse of Lisieux, St. Francis of Assisi, St. Thomas Aquinas, St. John Paul II, and so many saints who've challenged the Church to walk in the tradition of Christ-like self-sacrifice. He points to Peter Maurin and Dorothy Day, who took the challenge of the Gospel seriously and divested themselves of wealth as they served the poor in New York City. He highlights the work of average people—rich and poor alike—who've leveraged their lives to build meaningful friendships through sacramental living. And as I read, I couldn't help but see the shape of Christ himself all over these pages.

Miller writes: "Part of the gift of the Catholic Worker's sharp critique of society is to help us see our world for what it is—for what the Church has told us it is. Dorothy and Peter refuse to let us put our heads in the sand and pretend the status quo is anywhere near the Gospel's ideals. It is not. The Church wants us to look reality squarely in the face. And this is good because we want to live as much in reality as we can."

Don't put your head in the sand. Look squarely into the face of reality. Hear this counter-cultural plea. Take the work of Dorothy Day and Peter Maurin seriously. Study it, consider it, and implement it in whatever way you can. If you do, you'll find yourself changed. You'll see the true shape of the Christian communal tradition, and you'll be inspired to resist the disembodied, artificial self-selection of the day. You'll find yourself desiring a deeper sort of Christianity, one that's devoted to and centered in real-life, flesh-and-bone, hand-to-plow community that defies social and economic strata. Put another way, you'll find yourself living into a Christianity that looks less industrial and more like Christ.

Seth Haines

INTRODUCTION

They called it the Hill. The priest at the little church on Main Street, for whatever reason, hadn't heeded the conventional wisdom that the homeless were to be sent to the shelter or charged with trespassing, and so a group of five or ten men could usually be found squatting on old chairs or milk crates along the edge of the property that sloped sharply down to the adjacent gas station. They all knew one another, and had for years—Bubba, Mac, Danny, Will, Ruben, Mike, Concrete, and others—many of them growing up together on the other side of town.

I lived nearby and started coming to the church most days for morning or evening prayer, and I would occasionally run into them. I usually got panhandled and slowly started to get to know them, whether I wanted to or not.

At first the interactions were relatively short and often, shall we say, transactional—a few bucks or a pack of smokes, a ride downtown, or maybe a hotel room if it started getting really cold. Some mornings those of us who were there to pray would have to maneuver around a couple of sleeping guys to get to the door of the church.

Over time, it became apparent that I was on friendly terms with at least some of the guys. "Oh, good morning, Colin," Bubba would say as I did my best to gingerly step my 225 pounds over him. Bubba was a cheerful regular and always professed to sleep well on the cardboard box underneath the covered walkway, in part because of the large stick he kept in his hand for protection, which he named Betsy. "No one wants to meet *her*," he'd say with his good-natured chuckle.

Many mornings after prayer, a couple of us would end up going with Bubba or Ruben or Charlie to the grocery store across the street to get them some breakfast before heading off to the rest of our day. It got to be a hassle to go to the store every day, so we decided to just bring some cereal to church. We set it out, along with the milk and bowls and spoons, and chatted for a bit. At some point, someone asked, "You aren't going to eat anything?" and at that point you couldn't refuse, of course—not without firmly drawing a line between "us" and "them"—and so it was settled. We all started eating together most mornings.

After doing this for a while it began to become clear that we were getting ourselves into something, though we weren't sure exactly what. However different we all were, the combination of common prayer and encountering the poor had, quite accidentally, made us into a little community. At some level, the few of us who gathered to pray—mostly graduate students at Duke University—were becoming friends with the homeless.

If we were absent for a few days, they'd come to our apartments to make sure we were okay. We, in turn, increasingly felt more obliged to consider their welfare. Both "sides" were beginning to feel a little responsibility for the other.

What to do now? We were vaguely aware that this had something to do with the Gospel, but the situation seemed so particular and even peculiar. Had anyone thought about this before, much less *done* it?

The Catholic Worker

And so we did what any theology graduate student would do—we took our questions to the divinity school library and started typing keywords into the catalog: "poor," "homeless," "Church," "poverty," "hospitality," "fellowship." It didn't take very long before we came across these two figures, Dorothy Day and Peter Maurin, who had founded something called the Catholic Worker movement.

And the striking thing was that they had met, it seemed, the same kind of guys we had and had the same conversations and ended up doing many of the same things. But they also had put a lot of thought into it, drawn largely from the depths of the Catholic tradition. They talked about ideas like personalism; voluntary poverty; "the little way"; "blowing the dynamite of the Church"; good work; community; and cult, culture, and cultivation.

Day and Maurin had, it seemed, built up a whole philosophy around exactly the experiences we were having, a full eighty years before we were having them. They had made a whole way of life out of it, which they claimed was nothing but the outworking of being committed Catholics in our day and age. And they authenticated all of this by testing it with their own experiences.

This was by far the most compelling model for the Church's engagement with the poor I had come across. Actually, it was the most compelling model of the *Church* that I had come across. I was (and am) about as white-bread as you can imagine. I grew up happily in the Minneapolis suburbs playing sports and Nintendo and had come to Durham for graduate work in theology.

I liked the Church and thought I knew a fair amount about it, but it had never even occurred to me to get to know any homeless people. But something about the situation I had stumbled into struck me as right. A church *should* have the poor gathered around it. The smell of pews and incense and the smell of folks who hadn't had a shower in a few days somehow went together.

For the Catholic Worker, the Church was not some theory—it was not just a set of beliefs or moral principles. Each day when I walked up to St. Joseph Parish on this little corner of Main Street, I could *see* the Gospel. The simple existence of that place, with its round of prayers and mix of characters, was the closest I'd ever come to Jesus talking to me. It was beautiful. It was only later when I discovered that Day said that the world will be saved by beauty.

Part of this beauty was not only taking responsibility for the poor as Christians, but, as Day and Maurin emphasized, learning that in many ways the poor were there to help *me*. So the goal was not "meeting needs," but friendship. The goal was a new kind of community, which the Church, they said, had always been meant to be. That's what this book is about.

Looking for Something More

These days, in my day job I work at a large parish in downtown St. Paul, Minnesota. A lot of different folks come through our doors, and the more I get to know people here, as well as people in other parishes, the more I am regularly impressed by the faith of average Catholics in the pews. No doubt, we have our problems, but I tend to think these issues pale in comparison with the simple fact that there are any people at church at all. In an increasingly non-Catholic world, if you are in a pew on Sunday, it is more likely than not that you *want* to be there and that your faith is important to you. There are vanishingly few "cultural Catholics" these days—people who are just there going through the motions like they always have.

We go to church not just because we believe and want to practice our faith but because we are *looking for something*—something that our everyday lives are not giving us. Sometimes without even being able to put it into words, we sense that there must be so much more to life than screens, online relationships, social media, jobs we often don't care about, making more money, or the general encouragement to invent yourself or find your own identity.

We go to church because we intuit that there must be more to the community we experience at church than various forms of "friend dating"—a beer here, a soccer game there, virtual community, and holiday get-togethers with other people who are just like us. We go because we somehow know in our bones (even if not quite with our brains) that the Lord is calling us to more than pew-sitting, family prayers, and "social service," however important these things are.

People ask me, "What can I do for the homeless?" I think it's because they suspect there must be more to what Jesus says about the poor than writing checks to charities or volunteering. We have all heard that following the Gospel is supposed to fill us with joy, and we rightly wonder if this could take us beyond simply being nice to one another.

In one sense we are relatively happy, and we put on a pleasant face most of the time. On the other hand, many of us are vaguely aware that we are sick of our own attempts to distract ourselves through another day by constant busyness, often-superficial relationships, and, yes, more screens. We are serious about our faith, but at the same time we fear that without the next beep, buzz, ring, podcast, or commitment, the boredom and despair we occasionally glimpse might jump out and swallow us.

So we come to church, yes, because we really believe, but also because we sense that the Church should have something to say about the fact that the shape of our lives is somehow not satisfying us. Churches, too, do their best to respond, and yet often struggle to break out of the mold of offering as cures simply more of the disease: low-commitment gatherings, commuter fellowship, virtual "connections," and yes, even more screens.

We are longing for the Church to give us a vision of life that is a compelling alternative to this status quo. Many of us have a secret hope for a whole alternative way of life, with a depth that corresponds to the seriousness with which, at our best moments, we take our faith.

This book suggests that the Church has always had a vision for this kind of living, and the principles that animate the Catholic Worker can help us rediscover it and bring it to life wherever we are. It is a life of regular common prayer, material simplicity, fellowship with the poor, good work, and real flesh-and-blood daily relationships, rubbing shoulders with those who are doing the same. It is a life of friendship, adventure, humor, joy, and learning to take God seriously but ourselves lightly. This book outlines this vison, explains it, and says why it is so deeply relevant for those of us choosing to be in the pews today.

Not Liberal or Conservative—Catholic

I am a convert to Catholicism. In 2016, I was received into the Church, having previously been a priest in the Episcopal Church, a Protestant denomination. My reasons for conversion were complex, being both practical and intellectual.

As an Episcopal priest, I had been in charge of the hospitality house that eventually would grow out of the friendships we had made at St. Joseph's. There we had tried, and to a large extent succeeded (while not yet Catholics) in, following the way of life we found so compellingly embodied by Maurin and Day.

Upon my conversion, I knew very well that the Catholic Church was not perfect, but I was convinced that the Church that was the source of the things we had learned from Maurin and Day must be the true one.

It shouldn't have surprised me, but once I was a Catholic, it wasn't long before I got the sense that my new coreligionists were trying to figure out what *kind* of Catholic I was. It became clear that Catholics defined themselves over and against other kinds of Catholics at least as much as I was used to Episcopalians defining themselves as not being Baptist or Evangelical or, for that matter, Catholic.

This was wearisome to me because I didn't want to be a traditionalist Catholic or a liberal Catholic. As a Protestant you always have to *choose* what sort of Christian you are, in part at least by making enemies of the kind you aren't. I had been a Catholic-leaning Episcopalian, but now I just wanted to be a Catholic. Yet it quickly became clear that there were various markers by which Catholics identified themselves—the things that made them "really" Catholic in their own minds.

For instance, some look for a Mass that is austere and reverent, and maybe in Latin; others seek a Mass that is casual and inviting, maybe in plain English. Some look for a firmness and passion for certain dogmas and rituals or, on the other hand, a flexibility and gentleness with such formalities. Some look for a rigidness about traditional morals in the Church and society; others want the Church to speak to those on the margins of these morals. Some worry about our society's marginalizing of the traditional family; others worry about its marginalization of the poor. We all know people on both sides of these divides. We all *are*, in one way or another, these people.

This need to choose a side seemed odd to me, especially in light of the example of Maurin and Day. Their Catholicism was rooted deep in the heart of the tradition—it grew from the same soil that sprouted the Benedictines and the Franciscans and St. Thomas Aquinas and any of the saints. They didn't ever seem to identify as liberal or conservative, or anything but Catholic.

And the difference was, I think, that they were *doing* the unflashy but radical things plain old Catholicism had always taught. They had turned their backs on the status quo by living the *heart* of the Gospel, and so there was no question that they were really Catholic.

On the other hand, if the details of our daily lives as Catholics are basically indistinguishable from the non-Catholic world around us, it's no surprise that many of us feel we have something to prove by our liturgical styles or moral emphases. But Maurin and Day majored in the majors and minored in the minors, and so Catholic was all the identity and all the seriousness they needed. No chest puffing necessary.

Radical Catholics

Another way of saying this is that the Catholic Worker movement is about getting back to our Catholic *roots*. This is what Peter Maurin called being a "radical."

Today, we usually think being a radical means being contrarian or denouncing the world just for the sake of it. But to be radical is to be rooted—from the Latin *radix,* a root—and so to be a Catholic radical, Maurin meant, is to be rooted deep in the essential traditions and practices of the Church. It is not to be a strange, marginal, or fringe Catholic—it is to be *fully* Catholic. It is to go to the root of one's own life and to be transformed into Christ's image at the deepest level. It doesn't get any more radical than that.

Maurin's call to be radical Catholics is what the Second Vatican Council called the "universal call to holiness." Sometimes today that is dumbed down to mean that just being ordinary is being holy, but it's actually the opposite of that. This call to holiness means that the example of the saints, the tough demands of the Gospel, the invitation to be utterly transformed and give everything for Christ—and indeed receive everything from him—are meant not just for a select few Christians, but for all of us. The Catholic Worker prophetically anticipated this universal call and was part of a chorus of voices that brought it forth.

The movement did more than that too. It articulated a particular shape, a specific set of practices, a way of life, that would *be* that holiness embodied in our world today. For the real question for us is not whether we should be holy—of course we should. The real question is, What does the universal call to holiness *look like* in America today? What should I *do* to be holy?

As clearly now as almost a hundred years ago, Maurin and Day's answer points us back to the root: small communities of common worship, lay leadership, local living, hospitality, simplicity or even voluntary poverty, friendship with the poor, and a serious, deep Catholic analysis of our culture. While this is not the only example of faithful Catholic life out there (and I won't be suggesting that we all must become Catholic Workers ourselves in any formal sense), the movement is instructive for all of us because at its best it is simply the practice of traditional Catholicism given fresh expression for our own culture.

In other words, our world being what it is, and the Gospel being what it is, something like the Catholic Worker vision is increasingly prophetic for those of us looking for an alternative to the status quo. While utterly faithful to the Church and its tradition, it is in some ways a *new* sort of holiness, necessary to meet the demands and complexities of a challenging new age. Or rather, as Maurin might say, it's a holiness so old it looks like it's new.

The Christian Adventure

Each chapter of this book focuses on one major part of the Catholic Worker vision. The book is not a history of the movement, but an introduction to and application of its way of life to our world. We begin by focusing on the theme of community because this is really what makes the Catholic Worker tick. Only if we get this piece in place first will we be able to see its other hallmarks as *aspects of the social life of the Church*, rather than as impossible individual moral demands. Subsequent chapters then explore these other hallmarks, giving examples from my own life of what they look like on the ground, showing how they are rooted deeply in the Catholic tradition, and describing how ordinary Catholics like you and me can put them into practice today.

This book is a call to an adventure. It's not for the spiritual elite; it's for everyone, because the Gospel is for everyone. And because it's the Gospel, the Lord knows that none of us will take it on all at once. Adventures are journeys, after all. They are baby steps for all of us, and no one is expecting perfection.

For while Christians are idealists in the best sense of the word, part of the genius of the Catholic Worker is its absolute clarity that there has to be a deep humor and gentleness suffusing everything we do. Laughter and silly stories and failure are the norm. "Judge not" should always be on everyone's lips. We have to live and preach and pray hard because Jesus is real, *and* we have to be merciful and jovial and infinitely indulgent with our neighbors and ourselves because, you might say, the point of the counsels of perfection is that we don't keep them perfectly.

But the Catholic Worker is an adventure just the same. You will come back changed, if you make it back at all. Like the Gospel, this adventure is not just an adjustment of something that we need a little work on, or a mere change in perspective. It's a total revolution.

For the truth of the matter is that there are no half measures. Christ, without exception, calls *all* of us to leave *everything* and follow him. He asks us to spend all of ourselves—all of our time and money and intelligence and energy—in loving God and taking care of one another. What else do we have to do before we die?

As with the Gospel, even if following this call makes a lot of things harder, it really will make everything better. Could we be Christians if we thought anything else?

1

THE GOSPEL AS SOCIAL FABRIC

Eventually we started calling our time with the homeless outside St. Joseph Parish "Prayer and Breakfast" (I've always been creative like that). The Guys (as we called them) kept coming, and so did we. A few people from the neighborhood caught wind of what we were doing and found ways to be involved, even if they weren't quite sure they wanted to be at the table with us.

Betty and Linda from the Presbyterian church next door asked if they could make grocery-store runs each week and keep the fridge stocked for us. I think that was when we started having eggs almost every morning. An older English couple from the parish would sometimes come and cook. Students from the Protestant divinity school at Duke heard that if they came to St. Joe's, they could fulfill their obligation to say morning prayer and at the same time get a free breakfast. Homeless people from the other side of town heard our food was better than the powdered eggs at the shelter, and they'd come on over.

So the breakfast grew, but not too much. Most days there were ten or fewer of us. We got to know a broad range of people, and we met a bunch of folks from the community who were not homeless, but who apparently thought common prayer was important and also found something attractive in our little daily, forty-five-minute fellowship. We did not seek anyone out; they just came. I hadn't known any of them before.

But very slowly—over the course of two or three years—this random assortment of people became very dear to me. They were the center of my social life. We had become a people where there was previously no people—a new "we." And this had been strangely brought into being, accidently almost, simply by taking up the practices of the Gospel. It wasn't an "intentional community"; it was just a Church community.

The fabric that united us, in other words, was simply what we *did* to be Christians. We originally just came to church for the liturgy—to approach Christ in the prayers—only to find that Christ had gotten there before us and, even before we knew it was him, had approached us in the poor.

We ate together, enjoyed one another, and got to know one another. And all this required that we share *work* (a theme to which we'll return): preparation of the liturgy, opening the church, getting food for breakfast, coordinating with the clergy for the use of the buildings, getting breakfast started each day, serving it, cleaning it up, showing newcomers (both homeless and not) the ropes, even putting our heads together about who would help Ruben get to the other side of town to get a driver's license.

A couple dozen people or so (both homeless and not) came to be the most intimate friends over a few years—not by having long conversations or heart-to-hearts, but by being connected by our shared commitment to the Gospel. Or rather, it became clear, our shared commitment to the Gospel was also a shared commitment to one another.

The Gospel had become our social fabric, and our community was solid because it was not grounded in feelings or in liking certain people, but in being necessary to one another's life project of being Christians. We could not perform "Church" without one another.

Kinds of Community

I say that the Gospel became our social fabric because the nature of a community is determined by the nature of the bonds that hold it together. There are, obviously, all different kinds of community. I use that word so much in these pages, knowing full well that it has become a buzzword and a dangerous abstraction, and so it can be used to make just about any gathering look shiny and bright.

In my time as a Catholic Worker there have been many who have come to us over the years saying they were interested in "community," assuming that's what we were interested in as well. Then Blake, one of our seminarians who is now a Catholic priest, would respond by pointing to the duplexes across the street, widely known as crack houses. "They're a community too," he'd say.

His point, of course, was that Day and Maurin were not interested in community just for the sake of community. They were interested in being Catholics, and they found they could not do that without other people.

We can contrast genuine Catholic community with other kinds of community that we are all probably quite familiar with (but not crack houses, I hope). Take, for example, today's secular American community, which is increasingly fickle and seems to dissolve as soon as it is formed. Indeed, many have said that we have a crisis of community in our culture. And from the perspective of this book, I think it's easy enough to see why.

Unlike the communities of most of human history, today's secular community is typically not defined by place, work, or ancestry. It is highly mobile, low-commitment, nonlocal, and often virtual. It makes heavy use of technology and, even when it is not restricted to virtual meetings or social-media interaction, often has for its bonds little more than shifting social or political opinions or the fact that its members happen to go to the same school or work in the same office.

In fact, increasingly, shared use of technology *itself* becomes a central social bond, as demonstrated by rooms full of high school students each silently "talking" (as they say) to one another on their phones, instead of actually *talking* to one another. Their phones don't let them *share* what they have in common as much as they *are* what they have in common.

Because these sorts of bonds are rather weak and superficial, such modern communities predictably shift and break up constantly, because when we find that others are no longer useful to us, we can simply "cancel" them.

Kinds of Catholic Community

We might think that any kind of Catholic community is necessarily superior to all this. But not all Catholic community is the same. Many of us will be familiar with popular expressions of it that, however well intentioned, don't actually amount to much more than its secular counterpart with some spiritual sprinkles on top.

We've all been part of this kind of low-commitment, often one-off, event-based sort of community, whether it's officially offered by a parish or spontaneously organized by individuals. I have in mind occasional gatherings that include book studies with bourbon and cigars, dinners and holiday parties at big houses, last-minute playdates for the kids coordinated over social media, moms' mornings with coffee or mimosas, large and impersonal parish festivals, or theology on tap at the local microbrewery.

Now, don't get me wrong; there's a place for many of these sorts of things (I particularly like a good parish festival). They can sometimes be stepping stones toward genuine Christian community, and I certainly wouldn't want to see it all go away. But my point is that if it's the only kind of community we have, it leaves us still far from having the Gospel itself as our social fabric.

For the bonds that hold this kind of community together are not the works of mercy or the Sermon on the Mount, but more or less the same bonds as those that hold much of our secular community together: a certain amount of expendable income; constant access to texting or social media; a comfortable home for hosting; and having your own car, cheap (and not so cheap) commodities, purchasable conveniences and services, childcare, and free time.

These modern bonds do not create so much authentic community, much less Christian community, as much as associations of people with sufficient resources to enable a certain level of shared consumerism. Because of this, in these sorts of communities, we don't actually depend on one another for much more than company, and these gatherings do not, importantly, easily include the poor (or even someone who might have to save up for rent this month).

And this, for me, was an important realization, because this sort of community is probably the dominant model today across all different kinds of parishes and all different kinds of Catholics.

Individualistic Piety

We'll come to more of the Church's true vision of community in a moment, but it's worth noting now that this rather impoverished notion of Christian community goes hand in hand with the way that most of us go about practicing even the more "churchy" or "religious" parts of our faith these days.

For if we take the community out of Church and put it in taprooms and chatrooms, and let those arenas suffice for the social aspect of Christianity, what do our parishes become? They become, inevitably, simply hubs of individual piety. Church is no longer defined as a community, but as that institution that facilitates each of our individual personal relationships with God.

Even if we do our praying at church with other people around, we do Church, you might say, together all by ourselves. We are in no way essential to one another's faith: we each separately go to Mass, we each separately say our prayers and devotions, and we each separately seek to become holy. Being a Christian simply becomes the practice of private spiritual exercises between me and God.

Like belonging to a gym, Church in this model becomes a sort of devotional club for individuals. We all come to one place to use the equipment and facilities, but the point is that I get my spiritual exercise and you get yours—and we don't need each other to get that done. We come to church, take care of our own business, and head back home. If we want to—and maybe even if we don't—we practice our faith more or less anonymously.

So the Church becomes an impersonal institution made use of by a collection of individuals who just happen to come together to get certain goods and services: sacraments, beliefs, moral rules, and even a "personal relationship with Jesus." These are all things that we can have without having to get mixed up in the messy business of anyone else's life.

Why Community?

But this is not at all the picture of the Church that I encountered at St. Joseph's, or, for that matter, the one that is given to us in the scriptures. In the opening chapters of the Acts of the Apostles, we read that the early Church

> held steadfastly to the apostles' teaching and fellow-ship, to the breaking of bread and to the prayers. And fear came upon every soul; and many wonders and signs were done through the apostles. And all who believed were together and had all things in common; and they sold their possessions and goods and distributed them to all, as any had need. And day by day, attending the temple together and breaking bread in their homes, they partook of food with glad and generous hearts, praising God and having favor with all the people. And the Lord added to their number day by day those who were being saved. (Acts 2:42–47)

Here, and in other passages like it, the Church is portrayed as (1) a *people,* deeply involved in one another's lives. Moreover, they are (2) a people defined by the *Gospel:* "they" refers to those who celebrated the Eucharist, prayed together, shared their homes and possessions, ate together, and took care of the poor and sick, and they did it, it seems, (3) more or less *daily* (for they were "*together* . . . day by day"; see also Acts of the Apostles 5:42). The Church, in other words, is *a people, practicing the Gospel, daily, together.* Being a member of the Church is meant to be a whole *way of life.*

What exactly this amounts to will, of course, vary from context to context, depending on whether you're in the city or in the country, whether you're married or single, whether your community is big or small, and even whether you're an introvert or extravert. Sometimes it will look like what I experienced in Durham, and sometimes it will be adapted to the rhythms of a rural agricultural society. But the point is that such daily communal practice, if scripture is any indication, is *essential* to being Church. If we don't have it, we'll be missing something absolutely vital.

This is why Peter Maurin called the Catholic Worker way of life *communitarianism.* He refused to relegate the scriptures' vision of Church to the dustbin of the hopelessly idealistic. Like those early Christians, he thought that the Church should be "a new society within the shell of the old."[1] As usual with Maurin, this instinct was merely retrieving parts of the Catholic tradition that (for reasons we'll explore below) had been sidelined in the modern world.

As it turns out, the Church has always seen daily community life as vital, even in the most important matters of personal holiness and salvation itself. St. Augustine and other Church Fathers stressed that humanity, before the Fall, had an original unity that was then broken up and scattered because of sin. This happened not only spiritually, but physically and materially as well, as the story of the Tower of Babel illustrates (see Genesis 11). Sin breaks up and fragments human community.

Because of this, salvation in Christ includes the *Church* as the redemption of human community, bringing bodies physically back into daily proximity. This is why the same book of Acts, in addition to portraying the Church as a fully communal way of life, also portrays Pentecost, the Church's birthday, as the reversal of Babel (see Acts of the Apostles 2).

Salvation is in part *constituted* by being joined back together in all the ways that we were originally meant to be a unity. It is no coincidence that the early Church takes shape by being *united* in one place, gathered around the Apostles and Mary (see Acts of the Apostles 1:14, 5:12). And it's no wonder that when they did that, "the Lord added to their number . . . those who were being *saved.*" Community is part of what salvation *is.*

The same thing goes for personal growth in our faith, for the cultivation of virtue and holiness (another topic we'll return to). St. Paul's letters, for example, are filled with encouragements, as Dorothy Day often pointed out, that we are all "called to be saints" (see Romans 1:7). And the vast majority of the apostle's letters are concerned with how to live with other members of the Church—the obvious assumption being that becoming holy is as much a matter of living the Gospel with other people as anything else.

Only by daily rubbing shoulders with our brothers and sisters do we find the grace and friendship—and also the frictions and forgiveness—we all need to become saints. We don't only need the sacraments; we need one another.

Community and Mission

Yet there's one more reason daily community life is so essential. I said in the introduction that what really captured me about the community that formed around St. Joseph's was its beauty. And this, I think, is an essential part of God's *evangelistic* plan. When God wanted to get our attention—when he wanted to call us, attract us, seduce us even (as the Song of Songs says)—he did not send just a message, or a set of words, or a rulebook, or an impersonal institution. His plan for the evangelization of the world was to send it a particular, beautiful *form of life.*

It is no accident that Acts says about the apostolic community that "the Lord added to their number." Evangelism is not a matter of getting as many people as we can to check boxes affirming their support for some abstract religious theory. It's a matter of letting people encounter the beauty of the daily rhythms of the Church, and then saying to them, usually more with deeds than with words, "Come join us."

The goal of the Gospel is for Jesus Christ to be known and loved. And the whole point of the Catholic Church is that it is the way to Jesus Christ—it is the way, this side of heaven, that all people can have access to him. Through the sacraments, the Word preached, breaking bread together, the works of mercy, the pursuit of holiness, friendship with the poor—and all this in daily communal life—the world is meant to be able to see, hear, taste, smell, and touch Jesus Christ every day.

But the community has to exist for this encounter to take place. That is why the Church is called Christ's body. So, while I said before that Christian community is a people defined by the Gospel, that doesn't quite go far enough. For, in the way I've been indicating, the people *is* the Gospel.

The Gospel is beautiful, and therefore, for those with eyes to see, it is deeply attractive. And because that beauty takes shape in a community, joining it is the way that we participate in the beauty and so become part of the beauty ourselves. This beauty is the way of life that Catholicism is.

So, while it is true that the Gospel must be "heard," as scripture says (Rom 10:17), the word that is heard is embodied in flesh and blood in the real world, just like Jesus Christ was. Or rather, the Church *is* Jesus Christ's flesh in the world today, and the very beauty of that community is how people come to know and love God. He gave us not only things to believe and actions to perform, but an alternative society in which to make our lives. The Gospel is preached only by being embodied in a people, and it is accepted only by being joined.

2

BLOWING THE DYNAMITE OF THE CHURCH

Over the course of a few years, and under the inspiration of Dorothy Day and Peter Maurin, our Prayer and Breakfast group found ourselves living together in what the Catholic Worker calls a hospitality house for the poor. The setup included about five of us grad student or seminarian types, and four or five of our friends that we had gotten to know from the streets.

I'll fill in the details of how we got to this point as the chapters proceed, but on this particular day it was almost the end of the month and I didn't yet have money together for the rent on the home we shared. Mac and Danny were not getting along, and they had just had another loud altercation in the kitchen, one brandishing a fork, the other ready to fire back with a pot of Oodles of Noodles. Later, that was the detail we laughed about, but in the moment it felt as if he was holding a bucket of gasoline in one hand and a lighter in the other.

On top of that, a prominent member of the parish, Chris, was on my case again because, well, frankly, he just didn't like having the poor around. He was always pressuring the priest about "what we are going to do about them." This was the moment when Tony, a good friend from the community and a regular at Prayer and Breakfast, asked me how things were going. I didn't have enough energy to put on a cheerful face, so I just started venting.

"You know, we don't do any fancy fundraising galas or anything, and we don't have an endowment. We've got a dozen or so donors, but most are as poor as we are. I think sharing the precarity of the poor is good for us, but man, it would be nice not to worry about rent. And you know I'm not gonna kick anybody out—the whole point is living together, after all—but I can't guarantee the next argument won't be solved with a fist and a knife instead of a fork and a pot of soup, and that no one is going to sue. And I know Chris just wants his version of what's best for St. Joe's, but I'm tired of getting the evil eye. It just wears on me.

"So, I guess that's how it's going," I continued. "There are just too many fires to put out, and it's worse because you never know if the next one will be the one to burn the whole house down."

This probably wasn't the first (and was certainly not the last) time over the years that Tony would hear similar worries from me. While he would empathize, he would also encourage me that, hard as it was, we were on the right path, which kept me going. For my real concern was that we had somehow gotten something in the Gospel wrong and that all these headaches and risks might be for nothing. Should living the Gospel really be so precarious? Was I missing an easier, cushier way? Here's what I was really saying: "I don't want to be a firefighter anymore. I want to be something less dangerous."

And then it struck me: being a Christian *should be* at least as dangerous as being a firefighter.

There it was, all boiled down to one sentence. It wasn't the first time I had such a thought—probably some preacher had put it in my head years before. But it only became real for me when I was confronted by a concrete instance of existential vulnerability—and was assured by a good friend that the kingdom could be found *within* it. I wanted a Christianity that would run smoothly alongside the rest of my life—one that would be safe. Tony pointed out this was like wanting to be a firefighter without facing any fire—without taking on any risk.

There are lots of professions in which people put themselves in harm's way every day: police, soldiers, medics, and the like. Soldiers and firefighters don't have jobs—they have lives of profound commitment. They don't have coworkers—they have brothers and sisters. And they live as part of a fellowship that makes the very real possibility of personal sacrifice not only bearable but a badge of honor. They are always preparing, always training, always vigilant—always in a sort of combat even when they are not in combat, aware that at any point they may be called upon to suffer much, or even give all.

Was I really saying I wanted Christianity to be less than this?

The Call to Holiness

This is a continual question—not only for me, but for the Church today. What does it mean for me to become holy? Is it something anywhere near as involved as being a firefighter? It's common to note that we are *all* called to become saints—that's the universal call to holiness. But what do we mean by that?

Our own answers, and the answers of our parishes, reveal themselves most clearly when we look at the habits on display in our daily lives of faith. I think it's fair to say, for most devoted Catholics, that we think holiness has a lot in common with that individualistic piety that tends to define parish life. Individual piety is an important expression of faith, but it is also a very safe one.

This individualistic, pious expression of faith tells us to be very serious about our Catholicism, but to fit it in around the rest of our lives. Say your prayers, get to Mass, practice frequent Confession, keep high moral standards (especially about sex), and maybe even do some acts of service now and then.

These are all good things—but this is a vision of holiness that leaves our fragmented, anxious, lonely lives pretty much intact. It keeps our faith safely sealed in the sanctuary. We still have the same jobs and live in the same places with the same safe houses and portfolios and insurance policies and polite friends as everyone else.

Of course, we're encouraged to talk to our coworkers about Jesus when we get the chance, and to avoid jobs that might be directly linked to abortion or pornography. But it's rarely suggested that because of our faith we might have to make any substantial change to the way we live. Most of the time (so we are left to believe) our temporal interests and our spiritual lives coexist without conflict. It's risk-free Christianity. And that's exactly what I had been telling Tony I wanted.

The universal call to holiness, in this estimation, is mostly a matter of our private lives and what we do in our free time. It's a holiness that's invisible to most of the world—not one that throws us into an alternative fellowship that might end up costing us. We have no idea what it could even mean to be part of a Church more dangerous than firefighting.

The Early Church

Tony was reminding me that there was once a time we did know this kind of dangerous faith. The early Church, after all, was born into a world that was often openly hostile to it, as we see when we read the Acts of the Apostles. The fellowship of the early Christians was hated and hunted, largely because in not worshiping the Roman gods they had opted out of much of the social and political life of their society.

In Roman culture, just about everything you did involved the pagan gods in one way or another. The Roman equivalent of a Fourth of July parade included prayers to Mars, the god of war, for the success of the army, as well as prayers to the emperor himself, who was considered semi-divine. You couldn't even have a glass of wine with your friends without making a small offering to the god Dionysus.

So when Christians opted out of these offerings, they started sticking out like sore thumbs—they were mocked as being hopelessly anti-social. And this was dangerous because, to the Romans, opting out of normal community life was a political statement as much as a religious one. Christians were taken as not supporting the emperor—they were even seen as revolutionaries.

All this meant that the Church was a visibly distinct society. They contrasted their fellowship to what they called "the world." And, as with firefighters, their membership in the faith could, at any moment, test their commitment.

As we see throughout the whole age of the martyrs, becoming a Christian certainly was not safe, and those visible, communal, daily practices of the fellowship could be both a liability and a preparation for what discipleship might cost at any moment. It's worth remembering that Christians in many places in the world where the Church is persecuted still face these dangers today.

Under these conditions, the universal call to holiness was a matter of simply being a member of the Church. The very nature of being a Christian meant that one was actively involved in the voluntary and sincere practice of one's faith. Holiness meant, as it does in the scriptures, being set apart.

Of course the early Christians practiced individual devotions and experienced inward transformation and moments of deep personal intimacy with God, but this was *part of*, rather than *in place of*, a shared set of visible practices that were the essence of Christian living. The Church came with holiness, as it were, already baked in. There was no reason to be a member if you weren't convicted that its way of life was worth dying for, because simply being part of the Church meant you were going to live the Gospel, which could very well cost you your life.

The Church as a Peculiar People

This was the vision of Church that Peter Maurin was trying to recover as the only kind of Church capable of effectively engaging the pagan culture of our own time. It was the early Church's *communal and visible holiness*—its corporate practice of the Sermon on the Mount—that slowly, over the course of three centuries, converted much of the Roman world to Christianity and remade ancient culture.

And Peter was adamant that only such a Church—not just a bunch of pious individuals, or on the other hand just a religious institution with political power—could engage and transform our own society. "If the Catholic Church," he says, "is not today the dominant social dynamic force, it is because Catholic scholars have failed to blow the dynamite of the Church. Catholic scholars have taken the dynamite of the Church, have wrapped it up in nice phraseology, placed it in a hermetic container and sat on the lid. It is about time to blow the lid off so the Catholic Church may again become the dominant social dynamic force."[1] For Peter, what's missing from the modern world is not traditional values, a sense of the transcendent, religion, or even God, but the social reality of the *Church* as a distinctive people.

Dorothy and Peter applied this call to holiness to themselves first. We will absolutely and certainly misunderstand what they were about if we fail to see that, for them, the Church is simply meant to be the heart of life. The Church is God's intervention into a world gone mad—it is a fellowship that pulls us out of the world and transforms the world precisely by being a place in which people could live differently *now*.

And for all its warts, the Church, the Catholic Worker is convinced, is filled with divine power. The Catholic Worker is entirely dependent upon the grace and truth of the Catholic faith, and, though it takes the name of a "movement," it is really nothing more than the Church at work. So it's impossible to understand Peter or Dorothy without seeing that they were simply Catholics who took on the Church's way of life hook, line, and sinker.

But rather than picturing the Church as an institution, or as a collection of doctrines, or as a place individuals go to pray—without denying any of these aspects—the Catholic Worker sees the Church as people set apart. Scripture calls the Church a divine "city" (Mt 5:14), a "nation," or a "priesthood" (1 Pet 2:9). It is a people with its own customs, practices, language, ethics, and even material culture—it's God's new way of life. In other words, it's a kingdom that the gates of hell will not prevail against (see Matthew 16:18–19).

In this way you might say that the Church doesn't so much *have* a politics (conservative or liberal or whatever) as it *is* a politics—it's an alternative way of being human. And the main thing the city of God does—what *makes* it the city of God—is to worship the true God truly. From this worship its whole way of life flows, which makes it different from other tribes of the world. We are strangers and pilgrims in a land that is not our own.

As a peculiar people, the Church's task is to be *faithful* to its divine way of life—not to worry about being *effective* in changing

the world. Or rather, as we'll see in subsequent chapters, the way
it is effective in changing the world *is* by being faithful. This is
exactly what Peter Maurin had in mind in talking about blowing
the dynamite of the Church.

Despite their popular portrayal, Dorothy and Peter were not
activists or reformers in the normal meaning of those words.
They were simply Catholics who saw that being faithful to the
Church's long tradition committed them to certain forms of life,
which also meant refusing other forms of life. We will see below
that the Catholic Worker is known for caring about everything,
from the poor to technology to voluntary poverty to working
on the land. And it cares about those things because the *Church*
cares about those things, as we see in the way their newspaper
continuously cited official Church sources.

This emphasis on faithfulness rather than effectiveness takes
a lot of pressure off: We don't have to fix the whole world—that's
God's job. We can just go about being the Church in all the small
ways that make up the fabric of our lives.

Blowing the Dynamite

This faithfulness to the Gospel is the dynamite that Peter was
talking about—this is the universal call to holiness in action. But
what has happened, in various ways, is that Christians have not
asked what the Gospel requires. Instead we ask questions of a
lower order: *How can I be financially secure? What's best for the
economy? What's the best way to succeed? How can I be comfortable and avoid suffering? What should I do to be safe? How can
we manage the future?*

It's not just that these questions are merely allowed or tol-
erated in the Church today as a concession to our weakness—
that would be understandable. Rather, with rare exceptions,

implicitly and even explicitly, these are the *only* questions our parishes encourage us to ask at all.

Notice that these are the questions that become natural when you're trying to make the best of the status quo. They became natural in the Church because for the longest time it was in *charge* of the status quo—the Church was an imperial power. These are the questions of those in control, and the answers are predictable enough: *Protect your country and your interests. Be as rich as you can. Get as much as you can for as little as you can. Demand your rights. Never stop working. Take care of your own. Build up your military.*

The problem, of course, is that these are not Christian answers. For those you have to turn to the words of Jesus Christ: *Turn the other cheek. Blessed are the poor. Not only do not kill, but do not even be angry. Give to all who beg. Sell what you have and give to the poor. Blessed are the peacemakers. Blessed are those who mourn. Do not worry about tomorrow. Receive the homeless into your home.* In other words, deny yourself, take up your cross, and follow me (see Matthew 16:24).

But here is the absolutely essential paradox: this logic of the Cross is also the logic of the Resurrection. True life only comes out of faithfulness, which usually looks like foolishness and failure. Even in our daily lives it is only these sacrificial practices that bring life and joy. Only to the extent that they are consistently put into practice do they also bring a complete revolution of life and priorities. And they bring it to the homes and communities and cities and lands that practice them.

In the early Church, this dynamite brought much of the Roman world into the Christian fold. But over the course of time, the Church, with some good and some not-so-good motivations, got distracted ruling the world rather than converting and serving it. If you want to rule on the world's terms, then

obviously the answers we find in the words of Jesus are going
to seem silly.

This is what Peter Maurin meant about scholars wrapping
the dynamite of the Church up in nice phraseology: the Church
had made the radical message of the Gospel compatible with
maintaining a worldwide empire. We made accommodations
and said that the really radical parts of the Gospel were only
meant for some Christians, but not for families or businessmen
or soldiers. Or maybe Jesus's words were meant for all, but only
in the private parts of our lives, not in public areas such as politics or economics.

A Revolution of the Heart

Part of Peter Maurin's genius was to be on the front lines of a
movement in the Church—a return to the scriptures and the
Fathers—that refused these fine distinctions: there are not two
ways that humans should act, one in private and one in public;
one for the ordained and another for the laity. Christ gave one
set of principles, and he said to go and teach all nations to follow him. This means that, at the end of the day, Maurin's vision
for bringing the social order to Christ is the same as that of the
early Christians: not a tweak of the Roman bureaucracy here and
there, not an attempt to make the empire a little more just, but
a thoroughgoing *conversion* of every individual.

Real social change can only happen, as Dorothy said, by a
revolution of the heart, and that means each heart. The Catholic
Worker has no other vision for society than simply for Catholics
to be Catholics, to invite others to be Catholics, and so to create
a Catholic social order. Its vision for society is for it to be the
Church.

But this, as we'll see, had nothing to do with a top-down, state-enforced religion. No one was to be compelled against their will. Rather, also like the early Church, this was to be a nonviolent revolution from below: small pockets of faithful Catholics who simply lived the Gospel and attracted others by the beauty of their lives—or rather the beauty of the One to whom their lives witnessed.

Peter's crazy idea was that this little way of the Church had the most radical social and political significance. Yet it is sometimes suggested that this view of the Church as faithful rather than effective is too insular, that it advocates abandoning the world and encourages Christians to escape and guard their purity.

But this is a puzzling worry because over and over again we find among Catholic Workers not withdrawal from society but people thinking and acting in deeply relevant ways. They engage not just with the poor but with all sorts of non-Christians who are committing to agrarian movements; fighting for peace (including establishing camps for conscientious objectors); harboring political refugees; advocating for the rights of laborers (Dorothy marched with Cesar Chavez); upholding the rights of migrants; protesting against both abortion and the death penalty; and engaging about as many other "secular" causes as you can imagine. These Catholic Worker communities tend to be filled with minorities as well as non-Catholics, and they often become the center of their neighborhoods. It is anything but a retreat.

Firefighter Christianity

Peter thought that the modern world had gone wrong because this kind of Church had disappeared. Yet he did not nostalgically long for a return to a time—say the Middle Ages—when

Christians had more cultural hegemony and the Church could be the great institution guarding "traditional values." Neither, on the other hand, did he want a Church content with being a private club for religious individuals, invisible and separate from the social and political world.

For Peter, what the world was missing—what the *Church* was missing—was a fellowship of saints, living unapologetically and self-sacrificially the radical message of Jesus. This is not a Church that *has* a social ethic, opinions on economics, or political views; it is a Church that *is* a social ethic, an economics, and a politics. In short, it is not concerned primarily with how it might contribute to society—instead, it is concerned simply with *being* God's new society and inviting everyone to join.

Of course this kind of Church isn't safe! Of course it's dangerous! You might die. But so what—do we not believe this is the way to find the fullness of life (see John 10:10)? The universal call to holiness is firefighter Christianity. That's the dynamite of the Church.

3
FRAGMENTED, ANXIOUS, AND LONELY

Bill was one of our first guests at the hospitality house. He was the sweetest, gentlest man you'd ever meet—amicable and easy to get along with. He also suffered from alcoholism for a long time, but he was one whose drinking rarely caused any problems for others, and so he stayed with us quite some time.

Bill was a middle-aged African American man from a small town a couple of hours away from Durham; he had grown up there happily among his large extended family, whose roots in the area went back as far as anyone could remember. As with most small towns in the last century or so, it slowly became harder to make a living there as a farmer or even to get by with jobs around town. So, like many, he had come to Durham looking for work some ten years before we met.

When I met him, he was a regular among the homeless guys on the Hill. No longer looking for work, he now spent his time panhandling and drinking the proceeds, like most of the others.

At the house, Bill's favorite thing to do was watch the old nineties' sitcom *Friends*—a story about six twenty-somethings living in Manhattan and the new "family" they create with one another in a new world where traditional families no longer provide the community they once did. Bill would watch all thirteen seasons over and over again. He knew every line, and the show was all he would talk about.

He was mesmerized by the sense of *belonging* that it presented in a world that had slowly stripped him of any. He was also fascinated by the Church community that was starting to emerge around the hospitality house. "That's y'all," he told me once, as we sat watching together one day. "Y'all are *Friends.*"

It would be easy to sentimentalize Bill and to see him as one of those poor souls who fall through the cracks. But this, I suspect, would just be an attempt to make ourselves feel better. Because, for one thing, the world is full of Bills these days—you only have to go to your local homeless shelter and look around if you don't believe me.

More importantly, we'd be wrong to think that most of us don't have an awful lot in common with him. In fact, I tell his story because it seems to me increasingly apparent that most of us are just as lonely, fragmented, anxious, and desperate for community as Bill—we just cope with it in more socially acceptable ways. We are all part of a sprawling world of consumerism, technology, and bureaucracy that offers to help us forget our imposed solitude, a solitude that the very same world largely produced. So in this chapter I want to take a look at some of these cultural dynamics that increasingly make Bills out of all of us.

A Culture of Freedom

Why is community so hard to find these days? A useful place to start is the emphasis our culture places on the notion of freedom. That word means different things in different contexts—from free markets to freedom of consumer choice; there's freedom *of* religion and freedom *from* religion; freedom to choose whom you love and the freedom of the separation of Church and state. My point here is neither to be a cheerleader for freedom nor to point out its abuses. I simply want to note the fact that, historically speaking, this has been a big concept for us as Americans, and it continues to be so today.

For instance, we typically portray our political landscape with reference to freedom: those on the right often endorsing freedom of trade, freedom of religion, and the right of each individual to maximize that freedom; and those on the left emphasizing that freedom is a right for all and that it should be equitably attainable. We disagree on the *how*, but we all agree that the goal is as much freedom as possible.

The notion of freedom is closely related to many of our other prized values: independence, privacy, self-determination, and convenience. It's not too much to claim that these ideas are, historically, near the core of our identity as Americans. This means that we have as one of our primary aims in life to be able to get along *without the help of others*. That's what independence *is*. We spend an incredible amount of our time and energy, as individuals and as a society, maximizing our ability to manage life without other people.

When I take Holy Communion to parishioners living in nursing homes, for instance, I am regularly struck with how often they comment that they are glad that they can afford to live where others will care for them so that their children won't be inconvenienced. This sort of *personal autonomy* is perhaps our central value—to let each do his own as he sees fit and not get mixed up too much in one another's business.

If this is the kind of people we are, an important question is, What is going to bind us together? If the ideal is independence, what do we have in common *besides* independence?

This is a sort of ironic question, for you might say that increasingly as a society we are bound together by the ideal of not being bound together. There was a time within the past century when something at least vaguely resembling some form of Christianity served as a bond and gave us something like our culture's shared "common sense." It at least gave us a baseline ethic for public life, even if not everyone was a Christian. So for a while we kept together as a culture without really admitting that it was our Christian past we were united around.

Today—for good and for ill—that is increasingly not the case. And this has meant, of course, that we have had to look elsewhere for our cultural common ground. We've had a hole to fill.

Technology of Isolation

Over the last century, and more intensely in the last forty years, this hole has been increasingly filled by the role of technology in our lives. It's what we have in common; it's what we agree on; it's our common language. It's the first thing we run to when we've got a problem or when we're anxious or lonely. We continue to build a society where technology-based institutions and goals dominate. We've come to live in an increasingly mechanical world where the solution to every problem is more engineering and greater control, put to the purpose (ironically) of *increasing our personal autonomy.*

The boom in technology fits exactly with our cultural love of freedom. When cultural Christianity was removed, the hole was filled, to a great extent, by the cultural project of creating as many "freedom devices" as we could manage. The further irony is that these means of freedom now exercise a significant amount of control over our lives. We can't really get by as individuals or as a society without being *dependent* in a thousand ways on those who produce our devices, repair them, and keep them running.

And here is where we come to the community bit, because one of the most important aspects of our technological society is the way that it breaks up the social body and isolates us. There's a reason we don't know our neighbors well: our technology is not built for it. Our technology is built for independence and convenience, not socialization and in-person relationships. The mechanization of our society has profoundly *fragmented* us, and this is perhaps the main reason that we are more anxious, lonely, and atomized than ever.

Rules, Screens, and Money

This is the basic dynamic that I want to explore in more detail throughout the rest of this chapter. On the one hand, that technology fragments us seems counterintuitive because we are now *connected* and, as I've said, *dependent* in a thousand ways we never were before. We are more *electronically* connected to one another, and we are more dependent on the producers of our technology. On the other hand, this kind of connection has come, as we shall see, at the cost of *personal* connections and local communities. Every new gadget is designed to make us more *free* to live life on our *own terms*.

And so, after a million cultural changes with this goal, it's no surprise that we don't need other people anymore. I wanted a life I could do by myself, and I got it. I'm alone. When I do need others, I can pay for their time or services, preferring the impersonal and contractual, because in a way it preserves my independence. One stranger will do my laundry, another will take care of my kids, a third will drive me around. Even my friends I can "manage" online. So what remains between us are endless bureaucratic rules, mediated by screens and money. That's our current social fabric.

The motor that drives the advance of technology is our consumer society. New technologies are developed because they sell, and technology in turn is now the driving component of consumerism. And this too is related to community, for at the core of consumer society is *competition* with one another. We compete for jobs, for wages, for getting at the lowest price, for selling at the highest price, for job credentials, for the most influential advertising, for "cornering the market," for the best schools for our children, and for just about everything else.

Competition is just another way of saying that there is a significant respect in which we are *opposed to one another*. For we are all trying to get what the other has. But this means that there is always a sense that we are in conflict with our neighbors. This dynamic stitches isolation deep into both the practical and the psychological fabric of our lives.

As Christians, we should be suspicious of an attitude toward money and possessions that does not put them in some fundamental sense—as was the case for the early Church—at the service of the community, and especially the poor. But I, at least, grew up being positively encouraged to get whatever I could out of what I had, no matter where it came from. We often say, "It's just business—don't take it personally." But what if most of life operates as a competition? If that's the case, then one thing at least will be for sure: it *won't* be personal. Most of our relationships are now nothing more than one bank accounting with another.

Loss of Real Communities and Pursuit of the Common Good

This technologically dependent way of life is especially detrimental to small communities like those Bill came from. The vast marketing and adoption of all our new technologies, from cars to computers to phones, have gone a long way toward melding the whole world into a single, universal-but-atomized monoculture. But this has meant the disappearance of particular communities and local cultures that, until recently, were the normal building blocks of larger societies.

For instance, a century ago here in St. Paul, Minnesota, the Irish, the Germans, and the Italians each had many of their own ways of conducting life and their own ways of seeing the world. These were, largely, ethnic Catholic communities. They were far from perfect and had many problems of their own, but they were true communities in a way that surpasses most of our experience today. They had a thick sense of community because they saw themselves as a people distinct from others and had a consciousness that they shared a way of life *together,* rather than being a loose assortment of individuals. They knew they were involved in the pursuit of a *common good.* We are swiftly losing the ability even to imagine what such communities were like, and so it's worth dwelling a bit on what made them different.

To seek a common good is to engage in corporate actions—let's call them projects—that seek after shared goals for a community. Things like restaurants, schools, orchestras, libraries, sports teams, grocery co-ops, or family farms all pursue the common good. The common good in this sense is not simply cooperation so that each person can achieve his or her *own* goals more effectively. It's the opposite of that. The common good is a good that can only be *shared.*

Take a community garden as an example. Learning teamwork, establishing a sense of place, getting to know your neighbors, making friends, building trust, and participating in local traditions are all *common* goods. That is, you can't have them unless, in the having, you share them with others. Participating in the local project—being a member of a community—is part of the very nature of what the garden produces.

And this means that, as you participate in the garden project, if you want those common goods, your goals must become the goals of the community—they must become shared. This is a big part of what bound old ethnic communities tightly together, because to share goals with other people is *to become a particular sort of person yourself.*

For the garden to be successful, everyone will have to share responsibility for maintaining it. You can't plant seeds in May and disappear until it's time to harvest in August. You have to be ready to get your hands dirty, and you have to be reliable when it's your week to water and weed. You'll probably have to get to know others, learn from their experiences, and be humble enough to be a team player. The common good always involves shared projects, which involve shared goals, which create a community of a particular character.

In Catholic language, we are talking about *shared habits and virtues.* In fact, if a member of the project does pursue his *own* goals, which are not common, he will *not* be able to achieve the *common* goals as well. If someone decides she will do as little work as possible but still share in the produce, she will thereby exclude herself from many of the common goods listed above and will be an outsider to the community.

A hundred years ago, it was typical of local ethnic communities that they would be engaged in a wide variety of these projects at the same time. They owned restaurants, established day cares, helped run their parishes, organized fall festivals, and so on. In such cases, a rich and complex sense of the common good emerges, which necessarily produces people with the dispositions and character suited to these goals. Rich and complex communities were the result, which, precisely because of their own projects, allowed these communities to achieve a relatively high degree of practical independence. The community internally produced much of their own food and education and entertainment and culture and so on. They made their world a place to belong.

Fragmentation

I'm saying all of this to help us understand why we have so little true community today—why we are so fragmented and alone. For it is sometimes said that these kinds of ethnic communities were old-fashioned, so "of course" they don't exist today. But their disappearance has been anything but natural. They have not slowly decayed on their own, but rather rapidly dissolved as they were drawn into the life of modern consumerism and technology.

One of the central dynamics of our modern way of life is that it can tempt such communities toward making choices that are not for their common good. Instead of asking how any given course of action will affect the community—what's best for my friends and relatives and the neighborhood and the Church—consumerism asks me to base my actions only upon what *I* want and how much *I* can get for as little as possible.

It's hard to overestimate the hold this way of thinking has on our whole way of life and common sense. It has come to seem natural to all of us. It comes out in the short term and in the apparently trivial—we buy meat from the SuperStore instead of from the local farmer because it's cheaper. But it also shows up in places that reveal it as part of our whole life philosophy, as in the common practice of choosing a college far away from my community because it will help me make more money. It's good for me in terms of cash, but it breaks up the community.

But what we often don't notice is that in between the apparently trivial and the more profound a whole new order of values has taken hold of us (and notice that the way we talk about the moral life— "values"—is itself a consumer term). The goods we look to are no longer internal to a small community, binding it together, but "out there," wherever the best offer is. And so each of us pursues his or her own interests, and we are fragmented. If we keep doing this throughout our life, we never commit to belonging anywhere, because there always might be a better deal somewhere else.

Just like in the community garden project, this turn away from the common good is actually a transformation of our desires—it's a cultivation of different virtues and vices, so that in being fragmented we are actually *becoming different people.* Once we considered the community, the Church, and others in our decisions; now I am more and more concerned about myself.

And this plays itself out across our society. The next new thing is always supplanting the last, and so we live in the midst of a sort of perpetual cultural revolution. Older communities are broken up, and new ones can't even get a foothold before the next round of new comes in so that we have something else to buy. There's no place to belong even if we wanted to.

With each turn in the cultural revolution come mini personal revolutions for each of us, as we are asked to become the sort of person who desires what is *now* on offer. There is always something new on offer, without any reference to community, which creates constant pressure to reinvent ourselves. No wonder we are lonely and anxious.

One important consequence of our isolation is that we now have to look outside the local community for the staples of life. And this, after all, is what the entire apparatus of modern technology and bureaucracy is for: to help us manage life (the life it helped create) without other people, at least without any people we are not contractually obligated to. The once-internal bonds of local community are now transferred to external agencies and strangers, which are supposed to give us more freedom to direct our lives the way that we want. In practice, of course, the cost is an extraordinary degree of dependence on impersonal institutions and services. At the same time, we lose all those relationships that were once naturally embedded in everyday life. Having friends now becomes one more thing to manage, rather than something that simply comes with being alive.

By now, of course, most of us are simply born into this world. We can't imagine anything else. Cars, personal computers, smartphones, fast-food delivery, Uber, day cares, and a thousand other solutions are things that few of us could imagine doing without. They are increasingly the only social bonds that we have, bonds that paradoxically keep us isolated.

My phone allows me to stay "connected" to a hundred people every day and, at the same time, makes it possible to get along without ever being face-to-face with any of them. Uber saves the inconvenience of coordinating rides, but takes away the time to chat in the car. With the touch of an app, I can get food delivered, but at the cost of living in a culture—the first ever known—where families no longer cook together every night. And all the time we save from all these conveniences we can put to use to do . . . what? Invent more conveniences? So we have more time to watch our screens to distract us from the fact that we feel alone in the world?

Saving Bill

One day I got a call that Bill had been taken to the hospital. He had been found unresponsive in his room, and when I got to the hospital he didn't remember who I was. The diagnosis was that for at least a week he had had no food and no water, but plenty of booze, and this had put so many toxins in his system that he had, more or less, lost his mind. Some of his memory eventually came back, and his sister, whom he had not talked to in years, came and got him and took him back to their hometown to care for him. That was the last time I saw or heard from him. We eventually lost touch with the family, but his condition had not substantially improved.

Bill's story is a very sad one, but it is one, as I suggested, that increasingly fits all of us. He came from a place that once was a thriving community and in which he was happy and healthy. Through forces largely beyond his control, that community was fragmented, and he found himself a wandering soul longing for real friends but not knowing how or where to find them. He constantly medicated himself to treat a disease that was primarily of social, communal, and even spiritual origin. But he became even more addicted to his screen than he was to his self-medication, chasing what his heart really needed, which meant he was ultimately searching for real life in fake life.

In light of the cultural dynamics we've sketched in this chapter, it's not hard to see that our lot is the same as Bill's. All our communities are broken. We are all homeless, even if we're not homeless. And we all secretly long for real friends, but don't know how to find them. We might not be alcoholics, but more than half of us are clinically anxious and depressed and are medicating ourselves just the same.

We spend hours a day staring at our screens, sometimes imagining we have found there a real connection, but more often simply looking for a distraction from the horror of a real world that often leaves us utterly alone. Sometimes it feels as if we are about to lose our minds. We've got higher-class ways of doing it, but in the end we are all Bills.

This picture can seem pretty bleak. But of course that is always what the world, left to itself, looks like. It won't help at all if we are not quite clear about what we are up against. I would not write this chapter, however, if I didn't think that the Church ultimately has—and *is*—the answer to these undeniably serious problems.

For as we will see, in many ways the Church's very nature is to bind up fearful, fragmented, isolated—we can just say *sinful*—humanity and put it back together. The heart of what the Church does is called "Communion," after all, and she has been creating it where there was none as long as she has existed. And this she will have to do again, for in our time the forces against community are probably stronger than they have ever been. None of us who rely on what is merely human will stand a chance.

This is what Peter Maurin and Dorothy Day saw so clearly: kumbaya and hippie communes and socialist dreams and all the other secular attempts to rebuild society in our day have crumbled one by one. It is time once again for the Church to do what she was made to do. In this she is simply being what she has always claimed to be—the only hope for humanity. For we cannot live without community. It is the only thing that would have saved Bill, and it is the only thing that will save us.

4

DOROTHY AND PETER

It was the Great Depression in New York City. The year was 1933. Hordes of men and women roamed the streets of the world's largest city looking for work, food, a bed, and shelter from heat or cold. They had come, within the last generation or so, from the country's mostly rural population base, and for a time they found plenty of work in the newly urbanized and ever-expanding industrial economy. But all the prosperity of the Roaring Twenties now seemed a lifetime ago. There had always been poverty—most people throughout world history were poor—but this was destitution and misery of another kind.

How had this happened? What could be done? The range of political and social thought attempting to answer those questions was far broader than our political spectrum today. On the far left there was a live and active Communist party—right here in America—and on the far right an influential contingent supporting the absolute freedom of the market. Between and even outside these poles other ideologies jostled to influence public opinion. On the streets of New York City, newspapers, pamphleteers, soapbox orators, and agitators preached their solutions to the masses huddled along the Bowery or waiting for the subway. Men flew signs looking for work or a handout, or begging the government to do something.

This was the world in which the Catholic Worker was born. Such a scene can seem like another world—something we've read about in social-studies textbooks, but not something we've ever experienced. Yet, especially in light of what we've seen about the alienating nature of our social world, I would suggest that the difference from our own time is only superficial. The names, faces, and outward manifestations have changed, but the basic dynamics are the same: a once locally rooted population finds itself displaced by the advance of new technologies and the overturning of traditional ways of organizing society. Competition becomes the law of the land. The common good is set aside in pursuit of personal gratification, and once-vibrant communities are reduced to collections of isolated individuals left alone to face new physical challenges that drive many to despair, alcoholism, drugs, and worse.

Today many of us are able to avoid the more grisly aspects of such poverty, but all of us suffer psychologically, socially, and spiritually nonetheless. That was true then as well. It was a different historical era, but the same fragmenting wheels were spinning, producing the same lonely results.

In this light, Dorothy and Peter appear very much our contemporaries. What we want to do in this chapter is to get to know them a little better—not as abstract theorists from a bygone era, but as friends with a message we desperately need to hear.

The Founders

In 1933, Dorothy Day (1897–1980) was a journalist and a recent convert to Catholicism from an often-turbulent life as a writer and activist, deeply involved with the pressing social questions of the day. A year earlier, while she was covering a hunger march in Washington, DC, she had prayed at the National Shrine of the

Immaculate Conception for a way of integrating her love for the poor with her newfound faith. As a new Catholic she felt herself unable to support the kinds of radical causes that she once had. Her prayer was for a way to put some of her old life together with her new.

When she got back to New York City, as it turned out, an answer to her prayer was waiting for her on her doorstep in the person of Peter Maurin (1877–1949). Peter was a French immigrant, at one time a peasant farmer, who in his youth had spent time teaching with a Catholic religious order. He had come to the United States twenty years earlier as a homesteader, and he immersed himself deeply in Catholic social thought, philosophy, and cultural criticism.

Like Dorothy, Peter shared a deep concern for the misery of the masses. His learning had led him to develop a radical but orthodox Catholic analysis of what was wrong with the world, as well as a practical program for making it right. He had heard of Dorothy's literary and organizational talents, and he wanted her to help him put that program into action.

The first thing that they did was start a newspaper, the *Catholic Worker,* to be a means of spreading Catholic social teaching to the men and women in the streets. In this they were announcing that, just like the communists, the capitalists, and the anarchists, the *Catholic Church*, too, had a social vision.

The rest of Peter's program had three main elements: hospitality houses for the immediate relief of the homeless and poor, small-group discussions for the "clarification of thought" on social and political matters, and small farming communities where the unemployed could find good work. All of this, as we have said, was not, for Peter, a way of throwing the Church's weight behind one of the existing political offerings. It was a practical way of spelling out that the Church itself *was* the solution, *was* an existing political option, and that we Catholics have simply to put into practice what we already profess.

The paper was a hit, and very quickly a movement formed, centered out of St. Joseph House, the main hospitality house in Manhattan (as it still is today). Other houses formed, too, as well as other papers and a few farms, throughout the country. There were no official membership qualifications, and each local house or farm was free to embody Peter's ideas as they saw fit. Today there remain dozens of houses, papers, and farms scattered across the United States and even the world.

One of the good things about the movement's lack of official credentialing was, as I mentioned, the ability to be flexible; anyone could take the initiative and start their own farm or hospitality house or newspaper and use the Catholic Worker name. Indeed, this was part of the point: Peter was always stressing personal responsibility—the Christian duty and right to begin to simply practice the Gospel without waiting for anyone to say it was okay. That was probably one of the reasons the movement got off to such a quick start.

Yet, perhaps predictably, this freedom has also had a downside: it has meant that, as time went on, people felt free to use the Catholic Worker name without having too much that is *Catholic* about them. Peter and Dorothy were devout, even traditional in their faith, and it is only in light of their unflinching devotion to the Church—in all its official teaching—that the movement they founded makes any sense.

But it is true that today there are parts of the movement that don't share these commitments (it's easy to find evidence of this on various Catholic Worker websites). So it's important to stress that, for Dorothy and Peter, the Catholic Worker was never meant to offer an *alternative* to the Church in America, but rather one way that *the Church* can be an alternative to the American status quo.

Dorothy became the figurehead and face of the movement. She lived in the hospitality house in lower Manhattan for most of the rest of her life, and she traveled extensively across the country, speaking and visiting other houses and farms and reporting the latest news. She also wrote voluminously, for the *Catholic Worker* paper as well as books and other articles. When people think of the Catholic Worker movement, they think of Dorothy Day, and for good reason. An amazingly strong and holy woman, she now has a cause for canonization—the Church has given her the title "Servant of God," and she may someday be declared a saint. She died in 1980, one of the most famous women in the history of American Catholicism.

Yet it was Peter Maurin to whom Dorothy always gave the credit for being *the* founder of the Catholic Worker, as well as the holiest man she had ever met. It was Peter who really taught Dorothy the faith and instilled in her, as she said, a Catholic view of history, a philosophy of work, a vision of the poor as "ambassadors of God," the ideal of voluntary poverty, the dignity of manual labor, and the daily practice of the works of mercy, personalism, and communitarianism.

Peter was convinced that the only way to renew the social order was deep personal holiness lived out in community. And his life matched his mouth, taking St. Francis of Assisi as his model. He owned nothing, or close to nothing, and lived on the hospitality of others. Before he died at the age of seventy-two in 1949, he spent his time preaching on street corners, lecturing around the country, talking to priests and bishops about his program, and working on the land. He wrote dozens of what he called "Easy Essays"—short poetic summaries of Catholic social teaching designed for easy digestion—on anything from the pope's encyclicals to inflation to why Karl Marx was wrong. His program's vision, as well as its spirit, is well summarized in one of these essays, "What the Catholic Worker Believes":

1. The Catholic Worker believes
    in the gentle personalism
    of traditional Catholicism.
2. The Catholic Worker believes
    in the personal obligation
    of looking after
    the needs of our brother.
3. The Catholic Worker believes
    in the daily practice
    of the works of mercy.
4. The Catholic Worker believes
    in houses of hospitality
    for the immediate relief
    of those who are in need.
5. The Catholic Worker believes
    in the establishment
    of farming communes
    where each one works
    according to his ability
    and gets according to his need.
6. The Catholic Worker believes
    in creating a new society
    within the shell of the old
    with the philosophy of the new,
    which is not a new philosophy
    but a very old philosophy,
    a philosophy so old
    that it looks like new.[1]

A New Monasticism

Peter's program made sense in his fragmented, lonely world, and it makes even more sense in ours. For when people started putting Peter's program into practice, the result was the creation of a new kind of deeply Catholic community. People joined the movement in droves because they found there a compelling way of life, different from the rest of the world. In a world of boredom and isolation, people discovered like-minded (and sometimes not-so-like-minded) friends, meals to serve, prayers to say, Mass to go to, dishes to do, gardens to plant, alms to give, rides to give, doctor visits to accompany, errands to run, and stories to tell and retell. It gave you a purpose, an identity, a "people" (as they say in the South), in a world increasingly without any of that.

This inner life of the community was part of Peter's genius, often missed. He called it "communitarianism" to distinguish it from consumerist individualism on the one hand and from communism on the other. The model was simple, and anyone could adapt it to their own circumstances. Then, as now, it didn't have to be a huge project, and you didn't need anyone's approval. You could start it right now. It didn't have to be some grand endeavor. Then, as now, anyone could start simply with a small group of friends, or even a couple of families with children, with a place to pray, a pot of coffee, and some chicken soup. According to Peter, this was the way that we could start right now to build "a new society within the shell of the old."

Such spontaneity is exactly how Dorothy described the beginning of the movement: "We were just sitting there talking when Peter Maurin came in. We were just sitting there talking when lines of people began to form saying, 'We need bread.' . . . If there were six small loaves and a few fishes, we had to divide them. We were just sitting there talking and people moved in. . . . And somehow the walls were expanded. We were just sitting there talking and someone said, 'Let's all go live on a farm.' It was as casual as all that, I often think. It just came about. It just happened."[2]

The founding of the Catholic Worker movement, Maurin knew, was not the first time that Christians had found that they had to do something radical to rebuild a Christian life with others. In the third and fourth centuries, the initial zeal that was characteristic of the early Christian communities had begun to wane. Many serious Catholics had found that they could not live out the Gospel from within the normal confines of life in Roman cities. They saw that many other Christians, though they may have gone to church, no longer lived any differently than the pagans. We find the same thing today.

Slowly, small alternative communities began to spring up, largely out in the desert. We usually call these the first monastics or monks, but I bring them up here precisely because they were anything but overly pious, sentimental, or what we think of today as "monkish." They were Catholic laypeople who, like St. Benedict and like many of us today, found normal life degrading, lonely, and lacking anything better.

Communes formed that we call monasteries today, and families increasingly clustered together around them, forming one fluid community of lay, ordained, married, and single people, rooted in the prayers of the Church, in fellowship, in good work, and in hospitality. Far from a retreat from the world, these communities became so attractive to rich and poor alike that they grew into centers of what would become European civilization. But they began as simple groups of Catholic friendship.

This was exactly the way Maurin envisioned what the Catholic Worker was up to. Some people have called it a new monasticism. By that is simply meant that, just as the first monks were simply Christians readjusting to the demands of their age, we have got to find ways to do the same today.

"The Catholic Worker," Peter said, "is taking monasticism out of the monasteries."[3] By that, he didn't have any intention of denigrating vowed or cloistered vocations—he thought that religious life was, as it has always been, the beating heart of the Church. He meant, rather, that the Catholic Worker was giving

Catholics who were not in monasteries a way of practicing their faith in an equally serious way.

Still, calling the Catholic Worker a new monasticism can be misleading, because that might imply that it's not for everyone but only for super-Christians. But ordinary, everyday people like you and me are exactly who it's for: a largely lay-led movement of families and singles responding in faith to the challenges of our own age.

Peter's Program Today

By this point in the book you're already familiar with some important aspects of Dorothy and Peter's thought. They saw that authentic Christianity can only happen in tight-knit community, but they found society increasingly rootless and lonely. They saw the causes of much of this isolation in the way we have ordered our lives together. They knew that the only solution lay in embracing the radical holiness the Gospel calls each of us to, for apart from it we are left with individualistic piety.

In the next few chapters we'll explore several more aspects of this new kind of intentional reordering of our material lives:

- Personalism and life with the poor
- Voluntary poverty or simplicity of life
- Reconnecting with the land

Such reordering is necessary if we are going to go deeper in building communities with the Gospel as our social fabric. But it begins very simply, as the early Christians did, with a commitment to eating together.

5

CELEBRATION

Dorothy and Peter did not simply decide one day to start a hospitality house. They were promoting the idea in the newspaper, and homeless people started coming by the editorial office (Dorothy's apartment), asking where *their* hospitality house was.

Those of us in Durham didn't intend to start one either. After a year or so of Prayer and Breakfast, one of the regulars, Concrete (who was later to become one of my best friends), came to me one winter night and asked if he could sleep in my car. Eventually he transitioned to my spare bedroom. Then we moved to a three-bedroom place, and that's when Bill joined us. When that lease was up we found a place a couple of blocks closer to the church, and Mac (another regular on the Hill) moved in as well.

This was no strategic development. It was just what happened—I might almost say happened *to us*—over five years. I was going to classes and taking exams and playing pick-up basketball and doing other normal things in graduate-student life. And at various points the reality of what was happening at Prayer and Breakfast encroached one step further into my personal life.

Then one day I got a call from an acquaintance that a larger (eight bedroom) house was up for rent just a couple of blocks away. I called four friends who had been involved with the Guys in Prayer and Breakfast, and we pieced the rent money together.

The five of us, along with Crete, Mac, Bill, and a new arrival named Bubba, moved in.

As it had in several other crucial phases on this journey, a familiar question asserted itself: What are we going to do *now*? How, in other words, were we going to live together? We found Dorothy especially helpful here. At the end of her autobiography, *The Long Loneliness*, she writes: "We cannot love God unless we love each other, and to love we must know each other. We know him in the breaking of bread, and we know each other in the breaking of bread, and we are not alone anymore. Heaven is a banquet and life is a banquet, too, even with a crust, where there is companionship."[1] Every time I read this, I am impressed at the depth of what she conveys so elegantly in three sentences. Loving God and one another in heaven will be a matter of eating together, with Christ and with one another. That, it seems, is in some sense what we are ultimately made for. And so the Christian life, Dorothy is saying, is simply a matter of starting to live the life of heaven right here and now, by eating together. Life is a banquet, a feast. Feasting, believe it or not, therefore became our *practical program* at the hospitality house. It's the answer, then and now, to the question about how to live.

Eucharist and Feast

It starts, of course, with the Eucharist. This is the first "breaking of bread" that Dorothy refers to. Like all feasts, it brings people together, it unites and binds. And this is one of the Eucharist's primary tasks. We not only know God, but *one another* in it. This is because unity is one of the gifts the Church receives *through* the Mass.

Saving the world from fragmentation has always been one of the reasons God made the Church, and the Eucharist is his instrument of choice to accomplish that. It's true that the world is perhaps more fragmented than ever. But this is nothing new for the Church—it just means the Church has the same job she's always had in different circumstances. It is still taking fragmented, isolated, lonely humanity and binding it up into vibrant community.

I wrote above about projects—shared tasks of communities—like the community garden that create bonds, form character, and unite individuals. The Church's main project is the Eucharist. The *Catechism of the Catholic Church* says not only that the "Church makes the Eucharist" but also that the "Eucharist *makes the Church*" (1396). The most basic way that the Eucharist makes the Church into a community is by our praying *together* at Mass to become the Body of Christ. The Eucharist is the most important instance of a truth that stands at every level of our faith: if the Body of Christ is quite literally our salvation, and we can't get it without one another, then we are saved together. Just like the garden, Christianity is a project pursuing a *common* good.

This might seem abstract, but the Mass itself actually acts on our bodies in very practical ways to make us a community. There we perform liturgical acts in common. But these acts are not just one-off religious gestures; after a while they become *habits* that we incorporate as part of our *bodies* and carry with us wherever we go. And these new habits we get are *communal* habits, because most of the things we say and do at Mass wouldn't make any sense if we did them by ourselves.

At Mass we have to be physically together, materially in the same room, making the same bodily gestures, actually eating together, sometimes smelling the same smells, mouthing the same words. In a world of virtual everything, where you can be everywhere without ever really being anywhere, what a remarkable contrast that salvation demands this in-the-flesh togetherness.

And it demands it because salvation is not just a matter of going to heaven when you die, but of beginning the life of heaven now, as Dorothy says. We are saved *from* isolation and *for* community, even in this life. It's a thoroughly social matter, from the time we are baptized until, and including, the time we finally see God face-to-face.

As with the garden, then, participating in the Mass shapes us into particular kinds of people—a communal people. This is part of what it means to become Christ's body. The Mass "writes" on our bodies our very Christian identity: the life, death, and Resurrection of Christ. This habituation is the primary way we become more Christlike, and we cannot perform such actions or create these habits alone.

From the Mass, we learn that to say, "I am a Christian," is to name yourself as part of a physical, social reality. It is to say that your body is not just yours; it does not stand apart. It's a puzzle piece—useless and unintelligible except in its relation to others.

So by its divine habituation the Mass affects not only our souls but, just like acquiring other habits such as shooting a free throw or playing guitar, our bodies as well. We can think not only of neurological changes, but of the very way we relate to our own flesh and blood. As Americans, we find it possible to imagine ourselves complete as individuals; as Catholics, we only make sense with others.

The Mass actually changes what our bodies are. That's how practically it unifies us. And the communal habits that now constitute our bodies—that make us the Body of Christ—can't just be turned off when Mass is over. If the Eucharist is really the source and summit of our faith, as the *Catechism* states,[2] then the physical, fleshy togetherness we commit to there has got to work its way down into every level of our lives.

The Eucharist is the sacrament of *unity*. But it would be a parody of that unity if we applied it only to the time we're actually *at* Mass, or if we restricted it to some otherworldly "spiritual" unity. No: the *unity* that the Eucharist is the sacrament *of* includes the practical unity we see in the lives of the early Christians.

There, the Eucharistic feast translated into literal feasting. In particular, it became the custom, after the Eucharist, to hold a meal—they called it the Agape, or Love Feast—where the facts of the Mass started to become the facts of everyday life.

The Mass is a meal; all are welcome, because we all partake of it undeservedly; by it we are made into one; from it we receive our Christian identity. In the Agape, all this was folded into concrete community life: food was procured, prepared, and shared; the rich provided for the poor, including, often, the space for both the worship and the feast; people gave what they didn't need so that all could have what they did need; the problems of the day were discussed in light of the ritual they had just performed, the faith they had just professed, and the solemn vows of baptism they had just recalled.

In other words, they actually *lived* like they were one body, by beginning to make the fundamental tasks of life into Christian bonds. They shared, in short, as scripture says, "all things in common" (Acts 2:44), including relationships with all kinds of people. They were living the Eucharist.

And so today the most important task for Catholics, after the Mass, is just what the early Christians thought it was—feasting together: simply having some food, some drink, some conversation, without phones or screens, with a regular group of friends, on a regular basis. It shouldn't be a huge, gourmet production. Peter Maurin preferred a shared pot of soup and the kitchen table. Such regular meals will be an essential building block for remaking community out of the fragments of our world. And it's simply putting the Eucharist into practice.

Celebration

But before we *build* anything, we cannot lose the nature of these ordinary feasts as simply *celebrations*. Celebrations aren't for building anything—they are not useful or functional. Feasting is an end in itself—it's about enjoying one another, in the flesh, face-to-face, in the present moment.

This is important to get straight, because in the first place, the feast is *not* about community building. It *is* the community. Paradoxically, it *will* create social bonds, as long as we don't make it about that. You don't have to get anything *done* at the feast, and that is why you can *enjoy* it. Like the Eucharist, it is what all our other efforts are for; it's the climax of life. Bask in it. Soak up the good things about it. As Dorothy points out, it is meant to be a foretaste of heaven itself.

This is so important because savoring being together is itself an act of resistance to some of our worst ills. We live in a culture where we try to make absolutely everything—including other people—*useful* for some goal or another. But when this happens, when we are always looking down the line, we never see what's right in front of us. We never enjoy it. All we enjoy is getting stuff done—crossing one more thing off our list.

We do this, I suspect, because we are control freaks, always afraid that we must *make* every inch of our lives come out right by constantly steering everything to the *next* thing—what we think we want it to be. And so we miss the flow of gifts falling right into our laps.

But in the Mass, Christians have always celebrated the very opposite: the earth is God's good creation, given to us to enjoy with no need of constant management and manipulation. Every human being, likewise, is a little image of Christ himself—one of the main ways God is present to us. We are meant to be in awe of this, to be perpetually thankful for it, and to gaze in wonder at all that is, but especially the gift of one another.

So when we come to feast together, it is precisely as an act of conscious appreciation of the odd fact that God has put us here together *now*, for one another. In an ever-*distracted* world, by being with others we can offer our *attention* precisely to that fact—to our own unique *hereness* and *nowness*, which can only be received as a gift. Once we try to manipulate it and capture it, it slips through our fingers. But because it's good and because it's God's, we don't have to be anxious to control it. We can just receive our neighbor as a gift, without fear.

Our hyper-anxious world discourages us from doing this in ten thousand ways. It often rigidly, sometimes even violently, opposes this kind of simple acceptance of our neighbor. We are masters of suspicion. And so more than ever the Christian must insist on receiving the one who is seated right next to me, here and now—not for any plan, not for what she must be, not because she is safe, but because she is good. This is what Peter called *personalism*.

Laughter

Celebration, it seems to me, is also an antidote to what you might call the deadly *seriousness* that grips our lives. Traditional Catholic morality has always taken its own discipline with a healthy sense of humor, knowing that we are all sinners who, in spite our best efforts, will only ever be able to throw ourselves on God's mercy.

But here in our day, the world doesn't appear to be able to laugh much at all. This surely has a variety of causes, probably not a little to do with the underlying presumption that this life is all there is and so we had better get it right, and fast. It is a mad rush for pleasure, achievement, consumption, and experiences, because in the end it's tragic. Death is simply the end, so life is a war where we have to hurry up and get all we can. And the inevitable seriousness that results is killing our souls. We're not made for this.

So once again, Catholics have got to be people who plan light-hearted celebrations of all kinds at all possible opportunities. In this, we will seem to the outside world a people of a crazy hope, and that is exactly what we should be—romantics who foolishly believe our lives are not in our hands; that all will turn out right (and indeed already has done so); that even in the midst of suffering, good wins, and not just at the end but every day; that if Christ is for us, nothing can really be against us; that if we cast ourselves on him, he will not falter, and we will not fall; that the Resurrection of Christ was precisely for *us*, to make us as fearless as it did the apostles.

There is a wonderful scene that encapsulates this attitude in *The Lord of the Rings*. The story's heroes, Frodo and Sam, are crawling their way through the desolated, parched, lifeless land of the evil Lord Sauron, on their way to try to destroy his Ring of Power. They are beset on every side, with no consolations; enemies are everywhere; every step is an effort. Their task seems hopeless.

But at this particularly low point, Sam begins to reflect upon the bigger picture, seeing their current moment within the whole scheme of things. Someday, he muses, fathers may even tell their sons stories about them, and how Frodo had become "the famousest of the hobbits."

Then Tolkien relates what happens next. In response, he tells us, Frodo *laughs*— "a long, clear laugh from his heart. Such a sound had not been heard in those places since Sauron came to Middle-earth. To Sam it seemed as if all the stones were listening and the tall rocks leaning over them. But Frodo did not heed them; he laughed again. 'Why, Sam,' he said, 'to hear you some-how makes me as merry as if the story was already written.'"[3]

The irony, of course, is that the story *has* already been written. Tolkien is saying that for Frodo and for us, laughter—real, good-natured laughter—can be a way of defying the Dark Lord because it is an expression of the truth. The world isn't really what it appears to be, and the Enemy only has the power of illusion and intimidation. But laughing not only *expresses* this truth; it *realizes* it, then and there. It instantly remakes the world.

So, like Frodo, in spite of whatever darkness appears around us, we can—we must—*laugh*, knowing that this visible world and all its problems have been dealt with in the Passion of Christ. We laugh, not at pain, but from the joy that comes from that victory. We laugh trusting that God's good and already beautiful world doesn't require constant management, manipulation, or social engineering. The stones and the rocks—the very foundations of the present order—will try to intimidate us, precisely because, especially today, laughter is a kind of preaching the Gospel. And then we must laugh again.

Getting Practical

This sort of celebration, as I said, was what we landed on as our practical program for living together at the hospitality house. At first, it was really just a matter of allowing ourselves, over and over again, to have *fun*. Don't underestimate fun. It can lead to ceasing to be suspicious of one another, to ceasing to see one another primarily as threats, to ceasing to think that the best we can do is not inconvenience one another. Fun can help us to discover shared judgments, to refuse to unfriend or cancel one another. It can even lead to relationships beyond Facebook—to real friendships. And it is only in these real friendships that we can rediscover what you might call conviviality: the art of living together.

We discovered pretty quickly that making new friends does not mean we have to become best friends with—or even like—everybody we eat with. And this is a good thing, because it means that full participation in community feasts does not depend on how we feel. In our speed-dating and friend-dating culture, we are used to basing relationships on little more than sentimentality: whether we "get along," or have some sort of intangible "connection." But Catholic feasting is based on the logic of the Eucharist, where we know ahead of time that, left to ourselves, we *don't* get along. That is part of the point. We, educated rich white kids, didn't have much immediately in common with my poor black neighbors. It was not good chemistry right off the bat. This, again, is part of the point. It's not about our personal compatibility, but about our commitment to one another in light of Christ's commitment to us. These friendships are based not on what we know we have in common, but on finding the common that still lies hidden.

From Feasting to Living

Of course, if these are Catholic friendships, we may find that we have much in common. But after we establish that we have the same values and perspectives, these connections can come to an odd or awkward end. I mean, if we agree that we agree, so what? Most of the time, it means we then go back to our lives, take our fragmenting culture as unfortunate but the only one we have, say thanks for the soup, and then live by the same logic as everyone else. We may be of one mind, but in real life we live the same push-button existence as the rest.

And so part of the feast, perhaps not right away but over time, becomes a discussion about the way we order our lives together in other ways. We start becoming interested in the common good. And the good news is, given what we have said above, even this *discussion* of the common good is itself part of the common good, including its fumbling beginnings and all of the intricate complexity and negotiation and awkwardness of social gatherings. Feasting itself is an act of resistance to isolation and loneliness. And it is so because having any common good is a threat to the world, which thrives on turning all goods into nothing more than our private preferences.

Even among other Catholics, then—even if we agree on each and every point of faith and morals—we will still have to venture into the unknown of exploring the way that the Church informs the microscopic fabrics of our daily lives. Not just what we believe about religion, and what we do in the privacy of our bedroom, and how we vote, but fundamental questions such as, What is the good life? If we could build it from the ground up, what would it look like? What can we do now, together, to make life more like that? When we have come to this point of questioning together, we have come to what Peter called "clarification of thought." Then we will have to resist, once again, our usual habit of heading back home to our solitary lives, for fear of disagreeing or being an inconvenience to one another.

Concrete Application

I mentioned my homeless friend Concrete (Crete, for short) earlier. We'll get to know him better in subsequent chapters, but one of the dozens of truly amazing things about this man was the way that he had somehow independently figured out and, even more impressively, *lived* so many of the truths that I was only learning from the depth of the Catholic tradition and from Dorothy and Peter.

He was raised in the deeply Baptist and Pentecostal culture of the South and was probably baptized a dozen times but no longer went to church or claimed any formal identity as a Christian. But in terms of *living* most parts of the Gospel, he put most of us to shame. At some point in his adult life, he had made some sort of conversion, and (to put it in Catholic terms) he decided that he was going to follow his conscience meticulously, regardless of the cost.

One of the "Catholic" truths that he had come to in this way—entirely independently of any formal contact with the Catholic Church—was exactly what we've been talking about in this chapter: the absolute priority of the living, here-and-now presence of other people, including me. Being on the receiving end of such an attitude could be unsettling, both because of the importance he clearly placed on our simple togetherness and because, over time, he expected me to take the same attitude toward others.

He was offended, in fact, at anything less. That people could spend most of their lives running around occupied with trivial things like jobs and money and graduate school appeared to him a violation of what we are really here for. "People tryin' to use me," he would say, "and they tryin' to use God." But he was saying that neither people nor God should be used—they should be *enjoyed*. And enjoyed not occasionally, but as a way of life. "I can't function nobody" was the idiosyncratic way he put it.

Crete and I would eat together regularly. One night there wasn't a community meal, but, as often happened, we sat down to dinner anyway. There wasn't much in the house, but we pulled some leftovers out of the fridge. We used to do this all the time, and I wouldn't have even remembered this particular occasion if Crete hadn't mentioned it so often in later years to detail how much he enjoyed it: "That night we had those fried pork chops— you think you can get some more? Yeah, and that sweet red wine—what was that, man? I don't ever forget when we did that. I think about it all the time. That's communion."

Dorothy couldn't have put it any better.

6

THE POOR

Crete had not intentionally started living on the street, but once he was there, at some point he embraced it. This African American man in his fifties was highly intelligent, wickedly funny, and had the look and the sound of something like a cross between John the Baptist and a pirate.

When I came to know him, somewhere along his way he had developed, by repeated personal experience, a keen sense of the way that money, possessions, and power are so often used by some against others, and especially against the poor. He knew that in some ways even simply *having* some of those things might, often secretly, set us at cross-purposes with our neighbors.

Crete had, therefore, opted out of all that. He had embraced homelessness for the sake of others and because of the particular vantage it gave him on the world. And he would, if you let him, bring you into that view.

Yet that way of putting it can make it sound as if Crete was looking for disciples or had some sort of covert mission to fulfill. Hardly. If anything, at first he intentionally dissuaded me from engaging with him: he'd talk nonsense or knowingly offend my middle-class sensibility until he was satisfied that I was actually interested in *him*.

This, it became clear, was his way of proceeding with everybody. Only then, when he could trust you, would he bring you into the orbit of his life and experiences. He opened your eyes, but not by imparting any new ideology or theory. He wasn't perfect, but experiencing Crete—as nearly as I can describe it—was something like running up against someone who was somehow more fully human than anyone you'd ever met. And so simply by *existing* he called out everything he ran up against that was contrary to that.

One day Crete approached me and told me, as he often did, that he was "trying to get a little change to do this or that." More often than not it was to get something for someone else. "It ain't for me," he'd say. I was usually happy to give him what I had on me, but on this occasion it happened to be his third such request in twenty-four hours.

So I hemmed and hawed, and I said something about having to go and get something done (I should have known better by then that he'd see through that). It wasn't so much the money that bothered me as the fact that, this day at least, I felt as if I was being treated like a cash machine.

"Don't get mad," he said.

He wasn't apologizing; he was simply *telling* me that, as a simple matter of fact, I shouldn't be mad at getting panhandled. As usual, he saw the *real* situation with crystal clarity, and he was waiting on me until I saw it as well.

But I wasn't quite there. So I said something like, "Crete, I just did however many dollars last night *and* this morning." I felt like my dignity (or more likely pride) was being insulted, or that maybe I was being used.

So then he just broke it down very simply for me, in one of his great one-liners that put everything in perspective: "Man," he said, slowly and emphatically, as if he was reminding me of a tacit agreement he had assumed we had made, "I'm just trying to save your life."

In this chapter we'll see if we can get a sense of what he was talking about.

Rereading the Good Samaritan

In Jesus's parable of the Good Samaritan (see Luke 10:25–37), he tells a story about a Jew who gets beat up and left to die on the side of the road. A priest and a Levite, the religious representatives of the day, each come upon him; in turn, each passes him by. Finally a Samaritan—a stranger from another land—comes along. He stops, binds up the injured man's wounds, puts him on his donkey, takes him to an inn, and promises to pay for his expenses when he returns. "Go," Jesus says, "and do likewise" (Lk 10:37).

It's hard to overestimate the hold that this story—or rather a certain understanding of this story—has on our imaginations when it comes to dealing with the poor.[1] The moral of the story seems to be so straightforward: go, be like the Good Samaritan, and help those in need. This interpretation is so dominant and popular that it's embedded in the fabric of even our secular culture: we have "Samaritan" agencies that give out toys to poor kids at Christmas, and "Good Samaritan" laws that protect people trying to help others.

Yet what Crete helps us see is that this "go help others" interpretation gets the parable almost exactly backwards. The real meaning (as the Church Fathers almost unanimously saw) is not that we should be the Good Samaritan, but that *we are the man in the ditch. Jesus* is the Good Samaritan. Once we get this straight, everything falls into place—and Crete's one-liner makes all the sense in the world.

There are a number of details in the parable that point in this direction. The Samaritan is Jesus, first of all, because the Samaritan is a foreigner just like Jesus, who came to us from as far away a land as you can imagine—from the bosom of the Father—to a people who "knew him not" (Jn 1:10). Then the Samaritan comes across the "man" in the ditch, just like (as the Fathers noted) Christ came to "humanity" and found it in a terrible state: sinful and, as the text says in one place, "half dead" (Lk 10:30).

The symbolism then becomes even clearer: the Samaritan puts *oil* and *wine* on the man's wounds, just as Christ heals us with the sacraments—the oil of Baptism and Confirmation and the wine of the Eucharist. He takes the man to the inn—the Church—where he promises to *return one day* and take care of things.

Jesus is the Good Samaritan. He has not told us a simple moral tale about helping people. He has dramatized the plan of salvation with himself at its heart. And the result puts us in a fundamentally different posture to the poor than we have long assumed Jesus was suggesting: we are not the Good Samaritan; we are the man in the ditch.

This basic reversal causes everything else in the parable to make more sense. For one thing, it accords with the fundamental message of the Gospel that *we* are the ones in trouble and that we do not save ourselves. *Jesus* does that. He is the hero of the parable, not us.

For another thing, the "help people in need" interpretation implies that the *wealthy* are in an advantageous position in terms of being good Christians. Those who are able to help others get to be the Good Samaritans—they get pats on the back from society as well as God. In this interpretation, the poor, including the poor in the Church, have to be the *recipients* of "charity" and are likened to the bruised and bloody man. But that doesn't sound like what Jesus says about the rich and the poor elsewhere in the gospels. If anything, he paints the opposite picture: the poor are blessed, while the rich are going to have some difficult questions to answer (see, for example, Luke 6:20, 24).

Samaritans

Most importantly, this way of understanding the parable allows us to see the challenge in the fact that Jesus identifies himself with a *Samaritan*.

Samaritans, everybody knew, were the sworn enemies of the Jews. They were related to Jewish culture historically, and they retained some Jewish customs, laws, and religious observances, but they had mixed them with the pagan cultures around them. They were, therefore, in the eyes of the Jews, half-breeds: human, but only barely; closer to beasts and monsters. We see this negative view elsewhere in the gospels where the Jews insult Jesus by calling him a Samaritan (see John 8:48). *This* is the kind of person Jesus identifies himself with.

And this is why we have to start thinking about the place of the poor in our lives. Jesus comes to us, he is saying, in those we think we are most unlike. He comes to us riding on his donkey, or maybe on his ramshackle bicycle, in the person we most despise. Whom do we most despise? Whom is it that you cannot imagine reaching out to or having a meal with? Who are the outcasts? The "others"? The "they"?

Certainly, for our culture, the answer has for a long time been those at the shelter or living in tents or flying signs at the side of the road. Surely, there is some fundamental difference between us and them, we have instinctively felt. Surely there is something wrong with them. They made bad choices, or they use drugs, or they drink, or they have mental-health issues, or they were not responsible, or they are probably dangerous, or they were just less fortunate. *They . . .*

Not coincidently, then, elsewhere in the gospels Jesus identifies himself with exactly these people: the poor, the hungry, the thirsty, the homeless, and those in prison. He tells us that when we meet those people, we are meeting him (see Matthew 25:31–46). And, a point not to be missed, he identifies with those people *now* because during his life he *was* those people. He was poor (see 2 Corinthians 8:9), homeless (see Matthew 8:20), hungry (see Matthew 4:2), thirsty (see John 19:28), and in prison (see Matthew 26–27).

Jesus, then, is the outcast. He's the guy flying the sign on the corner. And the point is that he comes to save us today precisely in the outcasts of society we happen upon. As he bound up the wounds of the man on the side of the road, as he heals us with the sacraments, so the despised and rejected minister to *us*. Jesus is disguised in the homeless; *he's* the Samaritan.

But I am the man in the ditch. I am the one in desperate need of salvation. Do I believe it? Can I realize it?

Salvation means striving for holiness in every area of our lives. Too often today we reduce it to avoiding sexual sins and saying our prayers. But there is so much more to holiness than that. There are so many more areas of our life to which Christ wants to bring the joy and freedom of the Gospel. That is very good news. But the upshot of realizing that there is so much more on offer for us is admitting that, right now, we are in fact in *worse* shape than we imagined. There's more to holiness than we have imagined. I don't just have a few things here and there that I struggle with from time to time. I'm beaten up, bruised, barely conscious of my own condition. I'm dying, and I need salvation.

I need salvation from my pride, lust, gossip, lying, and the like. But I also need salvation from loneliness, from my screen addictions, from the need to control every detail of my life. I need salvation from thinking that salvation consists in keeping financially on top in the world by stepping on the heads and hands of those farther down the ladder. I need salvation from the wealth I've taken, often without even knowing it, from those who have less in our world of universal competition. I need salvation from the comfort I insist on at the expense of, and too often on the backs of, others. I need salvation from thinking I'm "basically okay." I have to see myself the way Jesus describes me in the parable.

I am the man in the ditch, and I am in desperate trouble. Who will save me? I've looked to the priest and the Levite, but they passed me by. And sure, there are "good," reasonable excuses for why they crossed to the other side of the road. But, in my condition, I need something more than that kind of respectable, middle-class religiosity. I've prayed my heart out; I've gone to the sacraments; I've done the spiritual direction. It's not working. I'm desperate. Who will save me?

Jesus, of course.

And here he comes, ambling down the road. Slightly smelly, braided hair, camouflage shorts over his pants. "Hey, man, I'm just trying to get a little change to do this or that."

Here is our Savior, staring us in the face. It's the last person we could ever imagine taking help from. He's the kind of person I secretly most despise. He's a Samaritan.

"Man, I'm just trying to save your life."

From *Doing for* to *Being With*

What Jesus and Crete are telling us is that we've got to get over the deeply ingrained habit of seeing ourselves as the benefactors of the poor. We've got to stop seeing *ourselves* as the ones who help *them*. Because most fundamentally, as the parable shows,

I am not here to help them; they are here to help me. I am not their benefactor; they are mine. I am not Jesus for them; they are Jesus for me.

And this takes us another step, from a fundamental posture of *doing for* the poor to one of *being with* them. Jesus said, in effect, "I am the poor." But, as Dorothy used to point out over and over again, he also said to the Church, "You always have the poor with you" (Mt 26:11). Catholic Worker hospitality houses, therefore, are about recovering Jesus's vision of a Church that more fully embodies God's presence by being a Church, as Pope Francis has expressed it, *of* the poor. This means being a Church that sees poverty, first of all, not as a problem to fix but as one of the conditions in which Christ comes among us. As Dorothy and Peter had learned from saints like Francis of Assisi and Benedict of Nursia, our primary posture toward the poor is one of *devotion* because in a mysterious way they *are* Jesus Christ. And the primary way we express that devotion is simply by sharing life with them. This is friendship with the poor. This is *being with*.

Such friendship is where the salvation that the Samaritan brings gets worked out in practical terms. It's where we can both become aware of and repent of the ways we need saving that we could never have imagined.

At a basic level, it's where my money, time, and attention can become the alms that atone for my sins: where my neighbor's poverty becomes my wealth. But it's also our path to holiness in our ongoing relationship with our money. It's where the popes' calls for a just allocation of the earth's abundance can begin, not in the form of some top-down communist scheme, but simply because my poor friends have legitimate claims on me. It's where we begin to live the Church's teaching that whatever we have beyond what we *need* must be used to supply our neighbor's lack. It's where we see face-to-face the ugly underbelly of our middle-class comforts, and we can begin to repent of our attachment to them because we love our friends. It's where those in the poor part of town can become "our people," where the world becomes so much bigger than "us" and "them." It's where we can finally be free from that gnawing worry that secretly undergirds so much of our lives: the fear of being poor.

Being with is where I start to make the organic connections between my bank account, my neighbors, and my community, and it starts to become apparent that we can all only be saved *together* because we can only be *good* together. *Being with* is a daily examination of conscience, as well as a daily invitation to the abundance of life that the Gospel promises, if only we will expand our horizons.

But *being with* is not just good for those of us in the middle and upper classes. Perhaps surprisingly, most of the time, the thing that helps those who are poor, more than anything else we could do for them, is our not assuming it's our job to help them. We can't, after all, usually fix other people's problems. What people of all sorts really need and want is support and someone to talk to—a friend to have a smoke with—while they and their communities work out solutions to their own problems. In most of life, so often there are no solutions to the problems we face, anyway, and our task is simply to laugh and cry and pray and suffer with one another. Or many times the problem is not really a lack of any *thing*, but a poverty of relationships. If you are sleeping on the street, it means there are zero people left in your world for you to couch-surf with. That's not a lack of couches—that's a lack of people. There's no lack of *stuff* in our world; there's a lack of *being with*.

Being with does not abolish *doing for*. It's fine and even a Christian duty to give alms to strangers, to feed and shelter them in a random, one-off act of charity, and never to see them again. Yet *being with* reminds us that all *doing for* is directed toward the life of community. *Being with* is the context in which the works

of mercy can become, as Peter Maurin suggested, the basis of a
whole new society. For the works of mercy themselves can build
community (as when Crete becomes my friend after starting off
sleeping in my car), and they can become a regular part of our
experience of that community (as when Crete panhandles me
three times in one day and I, in turn, learn from him what the
Bible really is trying to tell me).

This is just to underline the point that, for the Catholic
Worker, the works of mercy—*doing for*—are communitarian
practices. They are meant to function *within* tight-knit societies, or at least to begin to build them. Only very recently has it
become possible to imagine a dozen Catholics each coming from
their relatively isolated suburban homes, driving downtown to
serve a meal to people they don't otherwise see, and then going
back home—and calling that the works of mercy. Once again
this might be an okay place to start, but it's not where we want
to end up. Peter had in mind to make the works of mercy one
of the ways the Gospel simply *is* the social bond of our communities themselves.

Finding God

My encounter with the liturgy and the poor at St. Joseph's was
probably what kept me from quitting Christianity altogether
while I was in graduate school. It was where the Gospel ceased
to be a bunch of pious abstractions and *took place* right in front
of me.

An encounter with Christ takes place for us in the most
definitive way in the sacraments, of course. These are the
human actions that constitute the Church, and we are guar-
anteed that they make Christ present. Sacraments make us the
Body of Christ because in them we touch him, feel him, and

see him in the actions of *other people.* God becomes real to us in them because he is, you might say, impressed on our senses and imagination.

Being with the poor does something similar. Hospitality houses, or shared meals, or even just a few words to the man on the corner are the contexts that extend the baptismal font and the altar and the confessional. In the latter, water and bread and wine and priests are the tracking devices—the GPS—that allow us to see what God is doing. Likewise, in life with the poor, money, food, drink, rides, shelter, and visits—and the simple presence of the poor themselves—are the flashing red lights that Christ promised to use to let us know where he can be found. As in the sacraments, sharing life with the poor makes us the Body of Christ because we see and touch him in other people.

People today go to all kinds of extreme lengths to try to find God. We go on retreats; we fly thousands of miles to go on pilgrimages; we spend huge amounts of money to go to Africa and build wells and start schools; we perform all kinds of spiritual jujitsu and contort our souls in contemplation and introspection. And then we come home exhausted and, after a couple of weeks, call our spiritual director and complain that we still can't seem to get beyond our spiritual dryness.

Faith is not sight; but faith is closer to sight than we have made it. The Church does give us things to *see*—sacraments and the poor—that bring God experientially near to us. God expects us to believe without seeing, but he does not expect us to believe without seeing *anything.* The Guys on the Hill are not *physically* Christ as we will one day see him, but they are Christ enough for me to see now. Seeing them, I can believe in God. But if we've stopped using the means God has given us to know him, then it's no wonder so many are walking away from the Church. We have made Christianity harder than God made it by not looking for Christ right where he said he would be.

"Where's God?" so many want to know.

He's right here; he's *happening* among us, just like he promised.

There he is now, coming toward you on the sidewalk, trying to save your life.

7
THE LITTLE WAY

Life at the Maurin House (as we called it) slowly fell into a rhythm. The day began in the house's small chapel at 6:30 a.m. with Mass. Like all the parts of our day, it was attended by a variety of folks: most, but not all, of the not-homeless folks living at the house, maybe a few friends from the community, and every once in a while one of the would-be homeless guys we lived with.

After Mass some portion of us would wander a half-mile up the road to St. Joe's for morning prayer at 7:30 a.m., joined by still others—again on a demographic spectrum: some from other congregations, students from Duke, or just curious neighbors. As soon as prayer was done, maybe half of us headed over to the parish hall for breakfast at about 8 a.m., joined by anywhere from five to twenty folks from the street, depending on the day.

People pitched in for breakfast and cleanup wherever it occurred to them to do so (or not to do so at all), and usually by 9 a.m. most of us were headed off to our own day.

At 5:30 p.m. some of these same folks and some others— maybe twenty of us—were back at church for evening prayer, and then, two or three days a week, we went back on down to the hospitality house for open dinner at about 6 p.m. At 9 p.m. the bell would ring for night prayer, after which most went to their own or shared rooms, one or two on a couch, with one guy mad he couldn't stay.

Sketched out like this, it can look like almost a monastic ordering to the day, but as I've indicated, almost no one did all of it every single day. There were no attendance requirements, no one was taking roll, and folks popped in and out of things as they had interest and availability. We assumed that people would come to what they wanted.

Most of the schedule evolved practically and organically, just like breakfast did out of prayer. So, for instance, evening prayer eventually became part of the routine because, well, I wanted to say my evening prayers, and my dog needed a walk that time of day anyway. Dinners came about because, well, we were all hungry after evening prayer, and so we figured we might as well eat together.

In hindsight, what we had accidently done—none of us set out with any kind of plan—was a couple of the things that we've mentioned in previous chapters. For one, we simply let the logic of the Mass flow out into the rest of our lives. And so we ended up with a lot of shared meals and a lot of corporate prayer, which is perhaps not surprising given what the Mass *is*. And that gave us plenty of time to do the second thing, which was to begin to have those conversations about what should be the shape of the good life—the Christian life—in our day.

We talked around the dinner table, for instance, about the place of work in our lives, and that it should be something that practically unifies us, rather than just something that has to get done. And we came to that conclusion in part by reflecting on the Mass and the prayers, which are traditionally called the "*work* of God" (*opus Dei*). So if Christians find the peak of their unity in these liturgies, we figured other work should bring unity as well.

As a way of putting this idea into practice, after dinner we always invited everyone to help clean up and do the dishes. We did this not primarily because we wanted the extra hands, but as an open door to become part of the community—to do with us what we did together. To this day the normal American custom that guests *don't* do any of the cleaning up strikes me as slightly offensive—as a sort of refusal to deepen the relationship.

What all this illustrates for our purposes is the way that in such conversations and shared practices such as doing dishes—taken in conjunction with the rest of the daily routine that had slowly come into being—we had begun to establish a particular *culture* built around the Mass.

In the next chapters we'll look in more detail at why and how to build this sort of Catholic culture as part of Peter Maurin's idea of *cult, culture, and cultivation*. In this chapter, however, we'll focus on the *culture* part of that, which will lead to cultivation soon enough.

Matter Matters

Part of what can seem strange to us about Peter Maurin's message is his conviction that the material conditions of our lives have serious consequences for the practice of our faith. This was a truth he had learned from recent encyclicals on the social order, but it is not something that makes its way into sermons very often these days. We tend to assume that we can cultivate "the spiritual life" without much thought for our physical surroundings or the way they shape the habits of our daily lives.

Yet a central part of Peter's mission was about spreading the Church's message that the daily *setting* of our lives morally and spiritually impacts us and our communities. For Christians, it's impossible to separate the spiritual from the material, and this is built right into the nature of our faith: the logic of the Incarnation, as well as of the sacraments, is that everyday material is taken up into the divine. The way we relate to God is *through* the material, not outside of it.

So then, without reducing the spiritual to the (purely) material, there is still a significant sense that, for Catholics, the spiritual *is* the material. And Peter said that the separation of the two was the biggest problem of our times. In other words, matter *matters*.

For the Catholic social tradition, discipleship includes, for each of us, the slow task of trying to transform the material conditions of our lives into something more nearly resembling the kingdom of God. As St. John Paul II especially emphasized, we are summoned to the "evangelization of culture."

But when cast in such broad terms, evangelizing the culture can sound really intimidating. Are we being asked to somehow go out and impact the whole world? That sounds like an impossible task. So, too much of the time, we don't even get started.

That's one more of the reasons the Catholic Worker is so important today. Peter's program—played out in just *one* of its many possible forms in our little routine of life in Durham— shows what it can really look like to begin to evangelize our own culture by slowly and organically building community life around the Mass. We can really do it! The whole point is that you don't have to have a community *first*, and that it *has* to start small. The community is built *along with* the Christian culture. That's what it means to have a community whose very bonds are the Gospel.

This brings us to another possible obstacle to even getting started—the opposite one. Catholic Workers often talk about following St. Thérèse of Lisieux's "little way"—yet the little way of evangelizing the culture by doing dishes and eating with friends can seem so little as to be utterly not worth the effort. We've got kids to raise and bills to pay. What difference could these small acts possibly make in our own lives, much less the rest of the world?

And so the danger of discouragement can be very real in two directions:

"The task is too large—there's no way I can do it!"

"The task to too little—who cares?"

These are both feelings I have on a regular basis. They are totally understandable. Thankfully, neither is well founded.

We Fight the Demons

Providentially, during one of the many times I've been discouraged by such thoughts, I ran across a great *60 Minutes* documentary that I would often think back to when things seemed meaningless. It helps explain why Peter was so adamant that matter matters.

The piece was about Mount Athos in Greece, one of the largest collections of monks and monasteries in the world. The secular journalists who made the episode, with the best of intentions, were interested in understanding the life of the island and what the monks there did—you know, growing food, saying prayers, enjoying the tranquility. So in one scene the reporter asks a monk, Fr. Nicandros, who is out in a field picking olives and trimming the trees, what it is they do there. To which the monk, looking around at his menial tasks, replies, casually and as if it should be obvious to everybody, "This is an arena of unseen warfare. We fight against the angels of the dark side, the demons, the devil, Satan."

The reporter was understandably dumbfounded, but Fr. Nicandros said exactly what I needed to hear. Whenever our little daily routine from the house started to seem stale or

insignificant, I would just have to remind myself—and others—
what it is that we do here: we fight the demons.

Fr. Nicandros, for me, was a reminder that Christianity has
always taught that there is a lot more going on in the world than
meets the eye. The world is the scene of an invisible but real cosmic struggle that includes human beings and also those strange
beings that tradition calls angels and demons, those intelligent
spirits who are either the servants of God or in rebellion against
him. Satan whom St. Paul calls "the god of this world" (2 Cor
4:4), is the leader of the rebels. Our visible scene—the sensible,
physical, material world that Peter thought was so important—is
not separate from this invisible world or its battle. It is all part
of *one world*, with the material and spiritual linked together
in mysterious ways that revelation only occasionally gives us
glimpses of.

This is the key for our purposes: this unity of the spiritual
and material makes everything that happens, even mundane
things, full of meaning. Our actions, however small, always
involve much more than they seem, because all visible things
are outward symbols of a much larger spiritual, but really *real*,
intelligent and personal universe. We are always connected to
this world, so that our movements in space and time are movements on a cosmic stage. So, when we wonder why we are about
to get up to wash the dishes with the same people for the ump-
teenth day in a row, the basic answer is, "To fight the demons."

The Material Conditions
of Our Lives

Fighting the demons involves, of course, saying our prayers,
going to Mass, going to Confession, resisting temptations, and
the like. But we also fight them when we take steps to order our

material lives around the Gospel. For many times these material conditions are precisely the arena for battle that the monk was talking about. And they can make a big difference in the practice of our faith.

What are we talking about here, practically speaking? Perhaps a couple of illustrations are in order.

We've already seen the ways that consumerism and technology can undermine the community that Christianity presumes. These are important aspects of the material conditions of our lives because they are in many ways the motor that drives fragmentation. But they are by no means the only material factors standing against community today. As theologian Charles Moore asks,

> How would you go about destroying community, isolating people from one another and from a life shared with others? Over thirty years ago Howard Snyder asked this question and offered the following strategies: fragment family life, move people away from the neighborhoods where they grew up, set people farther apart by giving them bigger houses and yards, and separate the places people work from where they live. In other words, "Partition off people's lives into as many worlds as possible." To facilitate the process, get everyone their own car. Replace meaningful communication with television. And finally, cut down on family size and fill people's homes with things instead. The result? A post-familial, disconnected culture where self is king, relationships are thin, and individuals fend for themselves.[1]

Here, then, are several examples of the ways that matter matters: cars, TVs, big houses far apart, smaller families, and perpetual mobility all make living an intentionally Christian life more difficult.

The point is not, of course, that all these things are bad in themselves, or that they don't have their uses, but that, when taken together, they incline the very physical world we live in away from community and toward isolation and individualism.

There are, then, whole complexes, whole cultural formations of material realities—commodities, institutions, other people's practical habits—that have a real bearing on the possibilities of flourishing Catholic communities. We live our lives largely *within* the confines of these realities like a fish lives in water, and so we usually don't notice them. But, as with the fish's water, that doesn't mean they don't deeply determine our existence.

Or take another example: the way our material culture by its very nature tends to produce people temperamentally pre-disposed against the Church. It cultivates exactly the right vices to make Catholicism appear supremely unattractive.

Catholicism is old; it is based on ancient tradition. It requires a deep respect for the past, a willingness to slow down and be receptive of the teaching of masters and elders, to listen quietly and attentively to God and one another. In earlier times this sort of unhurried, tradition-respecting disposition was summed up in the word *pietas* (piety)—and it was related to both respect for parents and the ability to learn their trade as part of a community.

This true notion of piety, in contrast with the individualistic meaning it usually carries today, is a matter of docilely receiving the past from others as authoritative. That is why this virtue is essential for being a good Catholic, since we can only be Catholics as part of a living tradition learned from a community.

But what kind of a material culture do we live in? Not just one that is indifferent to a slow appreciation of the past, but one that is totally opposed to it—one that makes *pietas* almost impossible to obtain, even for the most devout. We live in a world charged with energies that propel us all—even against our best intentions—to love what's novel, the next thing, distractions, efficiency, and speed.

Computers, advertising, automobiles, lawnmowers, smartphones, same-day shipping, and the like all shape our tastes and predispositions away from *pietas* and toward what an earlier age could only have called *impietas*: the love of what is new, different, or untraditional, along with the corresponding denigration of whatever we were doing yesterday and impatient boredom with whatever we have today. We have, thanks in large part to our material culture, a fundamental distaste for the past and a firm conviction that the future is always just about to make us happy, and faster than it ever has before.

My point is not, again, that these devices are inherently evil, but that they are examples of how material conditions impact our faith, and the potential faith of the world, in a big way. For it means that, when you add it all up, as individuals, as a culture, and even as *Catholics*, we are often temperamentally indisposed to receiving faith the only way it can really be received.

And it's important to recognize that our world affects us like this whether we want it to or not. When we use and come into contact with these influences on a daily basis—as most of us do simply by going to work or raising our children—we are to some extent remade in their image. The habits and loves that they embody start to become our habits and loves. Who wants to spend time reading old books of dead men or sitting quietly in prayer when we could be checking out the newest styles on our phones or returning text messages?

Engaging the Demons

We have surfaced some of the ways that the forces of darkness are arrayed against Christians today in material guise. They are *persecutions* by our Enemy, such as there have never failed to be in the history of the Church. For in every age his goal is to do whatever he can to prevent the Church—as the main locus of God's saving work in the here-and-now—from being true to and successful in its mission.

These obstacles are not persecutions in the conventional sense, such as those we see in the New Testament. But they are just as real—and they are just as *material*. In the New Testament, for instance, it is very clear that Satan and his angels are in some way allied with some parts of the Roman Empire in harassing Christians and making it as hard as possible to practice their faith (see, for instance, Revelation 13 and 18). The empire puts Christians in jail, mocks them, kills them, confiscates their goods, misrepresents Christianity, and even feeds them to lions. The Roman Empire was in some ways the physical instrument of persecution of the early Christians.

Today we are in different, more subtle, but equally hostile circumstances. In our part of the world the demons rarely employ armies and outright persecution. And this, on their part, is part of their craftiness, for creating martyrs and open religious antagonisms is a complex and dicey business in supposedly secular democracies. To their own advantage, they have created the widespread (false) belief that our society is religiously "neutral." Do they really want to give up that pretense by singling out Christians?

And so they have learned better and more indirect tactics than they used in former times. It's much safer to quietly create in plain sight an environment that will virtually ensure that the real Christianity of the early Church can only be practiced with the most heroic efforts. So the Enemy orchestrates as many built-in cultural roadblocks to the faith as possible.

The Little Way

All this is the framework in which we have to understand the Catholic Worker's devotion to St. Thérèse of Lisieux and her little way in particular. Thérèse was a nineteenth-century Carmelite nun who died of tuberculosis at age twenty-four. As the saint herself recounts it in her autobiography, she struggled with how to reconcile her desire to be a hero for Christ and to accomplish great acts—to be a martyr, a missionary, a great teacher of the faith, out there in the wide world converting the nations—with her desire to spend her life at prayer in the monastery.

She found the solution precisely in the "little way of great love" that she was able to exercise in every moment of her day: to make sacrifices for the weaker sisters, to forgive, to smile at those she was angry with, to bear her sufferings cheerfully, and to do battle with the devil in the liturgy. She knew there was nothing neutral, that everything was connected, and so by these small actions she could *be* the hero she longed to be, one who was fighting, evangelizing, teaching right where she was. Actions might be small, but the effects were no less.

Faced with a material world that is spiritually set against us, we can be tempted to think in terms of big solutions—of power politics and "systemic change." But what Thérèse shows us so clearly is not that these merely political solutions are too high and powerful for a bunch of ordinary Christians doing the same things day after day, but that they are not powerful *enough* for us because they do not use the weapons of the Gospel. Polity and government have their place, but the only way the Gospel is really spread is by rooting it permanently in each of our hearts by living it out in the practices of each of our lives.

And the Catholic Worker shows us what Thérèse's message can look like practically today. We can begin, right in our homes, neighborhoods, and parishes, to tear down the material conditions of isolation, consumerism, distraction, and the rest, and to put in their place cultures such as the daily rhythm we slowly began to develop in Durham. If we want a true cultural revolution, it starts, as Dorothy says, with "a revolution of the heart": a revolution of cooking together instead of fast food, of conversation rather than television, of smaller houses closer together, of new friends rather than new things, of faces rather than screens, of feet rather than tires.

And so Thérèse, as Dorothy and Peter saw, invites us to fight the demons in our own little ways, in our own proverbial monasteries and lions' dens today. And here we will once again have to avoid the temptation to make this a *spiritualization* of the Gospel—as if the little way is about going around doing the *same things* with a different intention or spiritual perspective. Rather, if Peter is right that the separation of the material from the spiritual is the greatest error of modern times, and if we take the ways our society makes it hard to be the Church seriously, we should rather speak of the little way as the *materialization* of the Gospel. It's making a world, as Peter said, "where it is easier to be good."[2]

The bad news is that, as we've seen, we've got our work cut out for us. The good news is that every little step we take in this regard *is* the practice of the Gospel, *is* warfare, and *does* fight the demons. That's what the little way means. Every action is complete in itself, and even if it doesn't produce any visible result, it accomplishes its objective. In our prayers, in our meals together, in fellowship with the poor, in deciding for conversation and a walk rather than a drive or more screen time, in standing at the sink together doing the dishes, we are not just *preparing* to build a new society—we are actually living in it.

8

CULT, CULTURE, AND CULTIVATION

Bubba, whom I mentioned in an earlier chapter, was six-foot-six and two hundred forty pounds, almost always in a good mood, always ready to chat, and always ready to panhandle you. "I bet you didn't know I'm a professor of English," he'd say in his deep, *deep* voice.

"Really?"

"Yep, Old English [malt liquor]! Ah ha ha ha ha!"

He was one of the mainstays of the Guys, and in later years he would come to live at the hospitality house and become a real friend. But when I first met him, he lived in a tent in the woods, right across the street from the church.

I don't remember how the topic ever came up, but early on he said he would rather live there than at any of his other options: "People come in here, they say, 'Why don't you get a job?' Oh, what you want me to do, go work at the gas station, standing up behind a counter forty, fifty, sixty hours a week? Getting paid just enough to get me some bug-infested room all the way across town? Hell, no! I got bugs right here! Ha ha! You think I need to buy food? Hell, no. I got you to buy it for me! ! Ha ha ha.

"Out here I got everything I need," he'd continue. "The birds, the air, even Danny! I'm not going through all that shenanigans to be able to come out here in my *free* time and do what I can just do out here *all* the time."

Bubba had understood, in effect, that the conventional way of fitting into society was always going to give him a raw deal with demeaning and unfulfilling work, low pay, and meager living options. But he also saw that, even if he did somehow manage to climb the social ladder, at the end of his long days, when he wanted to relax and have fun, he would just come back up to the Hill and hang out with his friends.

Bubba wasn't buying it.

Cultivation

In this chapter and the next, we're going to be broadly exploring what Peter called his "philosophy of labor." That might sound like stuff for scholars, but it's really quite practical, as we'll see soon enough. Both of these chapters will help us understand Bubba's situation better and will put us in a good position to then see (in chapter 10) how our Durham community grew and stabilized itself by finding good work outside of conventional channels, even while we kept our "normal" jobs.

The present chapter prepares the ground for this approach to labor by looking at what Peter called "cultivation"—a reconnection with working the land that is part of our divine vocation. In the next chapter, building on this connection to the land, we'll look in more detail at the Church's teaching about what makes work good and why.

All this is relevant because, as both Peter and Bubba saw, so much of the work on offer today is, frankly, below the dignity of human beings. In Peter's day, that often meant mindless factory work, spending all day every day performing the same meaningless mechanical action over and over again—becoming the extension, basically, of a machine. In Bubba's day, that meant (and often means) much the same thing: standing behind a cash register, or a computer, all day every day, performing the same meaningless actions over and over again as the extension of a machine, and getting out of it a life that was in many ways worse than what he had with no job at all.

Peter thought the Church could do better, and so he called for *cult, culture, and cultivation*. "Cult," today, is sometimes used to describe crazy sectarian groups, but the original meaning of the word, the way Peter used it, simply refers to an organized system of *worship*. By "cult" Peter meant the Mass. By "culture," as we have seen, he meant a life built around the Mass. And "cultivation" is then the further extension of the *culture* of the *cult* to all of life, and especially to our *work*. It's the last part of a full Christianization of life.

Peter didn't think that we all had to move out to farms. There was plenty of good work to be found in cities, as we'll see. But he did think that each of us, as part of our faith, has a lot to gain from an increased consciousness of our dependence on the soil as the very source of our bodily life. Working the earth, he thought, was a divine *vocation*, common to all human beings. And he thought that each of us could do things in our daily lives, even in the cities, to put this vocation into practice. This, he thought, in the spirit of the little way, was another way that our spiritual and material lives are inseparably linked.

One caveat is in order before we jump in. In this chapter, I'm going to be talking about big differences between agrarian and industrial modes of life. But I want to avoid giving the impression that preindustrial life was wonderful or easy, or that if we could just go back to it, everything would be better. There were good things about it, as we'll see, but there were lots of problems, sin, and evil back then too.

I am no agrarian romantic, and Peter wasn't either. His point was not at all that modern life was terrible and that we should abandon it all and retreat into walled-off communes. We couldn't do that even if we thought we should. And, as we've seen, Peter's whole program is about *engaging* the modern world, not rejecting it.

The point, rather, is about *understanding* our world and finding ways to live more faithfully in it. In order to understand the unique character of modern work, we have to recognize, not with wistful nostalgia but simply as matters of history, the unprecedented nature of our industrial lives and some of the challenges and opportunities this presents Catholics today. The outline we give of these dynamics below is necessarily simplified, but no less true and relevant.

The Industrial Turn

The full significance of cultivation in the Christian life can only really be grasped if we first appreciate the seismic historical and cultural shift brought on over the last two centuries by the Industrial Revolution. As farmer and writer Wendell Berry notes, "Today, we like to talk about all kinds of revolutions: the fossil-fuel revolution, the automotive revolution, the assembly-line revolution, the antibiotic revolution, the sexual revolution, the computer revolution, the green revolution, the genomic revolution, and so on. But these revolutions . . . are all mere episodes of the one truly revolutionary revolution perhaps in the history of the human race, the Industrial Revolution."[1] What is it about *this* revolution that makes it the "one truly revolutionary revolution perhaps in the history of the human race"? To answer this question, let's consider a little bit about what went before it, in comparison with what we have now.

Before about two hundred years ago in most places in the world, and more recently in America, most of the population was occupied in subsistence-based agriculture and its related arts and crafts. By "subsistence" I just mean that whatever they grew or made was largely made for personal consumption, rather than primarily for selling on the market. You grew what you ate, and ate what you grew. If you made a shirt, it was usually for you or a family member to wear. By "agriculture" I mean that most people were farmers. If you weren't one, but worked as a cobbler or in carpentry, you were still dependent, usually in a visible way, on the land for your materials and also for your food. You were still close, literally and metaphorically, to the earth.

There were, of course, cities, which held all kinds of professions not directly on the land. But 80 or 90 percent of the population was living off the land. That statistic is today more than directly inverted in the United States, with less than 2 percent of people living off the land, and far less than that doing it for subsistence.

This, in a nutshell, is the one truly revolutionary revolution: from almost everyone living on the land, to almost no one. What I want to do now is enter imaginatively into some of the massive changes that accompanied this shift, particularly as they impacted faith, community, and work. We should keep Bubba in mind through all of this.

Community, Cultivation, and the Earth

The first difference between modern and agricultural societies is the way that *community* on the land is built into life itself. One of the things that I hear from many Minnesota old-timers who grew up farming is that they could never have done it—indeed could never have *survived*—without their neighbors. Family farms were not isolated from one another, but were in constant practical need of one another. Planting, harvest, barn-building, slaughtering, field-clearing, seed-sharing, and countless other tasks were *shared* tasks. Each turn of the season brought about another round of trips to neighboring farms and neighbors' trips to yours.

The requirements of the land, therefore, brought built-in friends, for you could not get by without them. The idea that work and friends could be two different things was unthinkable. Business and pleasure were *always* mixed. Who got along with whom was related to matters of life and death; the strength of the community was the strength of the agriculture, and vice versa. Community was created by shared work, and that work was necessary because it brought the necessities of life out of the earth.

Morality, Cultivation, and the Earth

The second difference between modern and agricultural societies has to do with the moral dimension of work on the land. The very fact that the earth demands things of our bodies can *make us different people.* For instance, farmers have to get up in the morning and milk the cows, every day, whether they want to or not. In Minnesota, they have to change the water in the chicken coop in the winter every day, or it will freeze. These tasks and countless others have to be done consistently, on time, and *well* if the farm is going to succeed.

Complex knowledge is also required. Farmers have to know their animals and their habitat well enough to discern when something is wrong, and that only comes with time and attention. They have to know what part of their fields can be planted with which seed, which animals should graze on it when, when it should be tilled in the spring, and how each field is best protected in the winter. This kind of knowledge is intimate knowledge of a very particular place, which by definition cannot be learned from books because it is the knowledge of a *place* that is not every place. It only comes from experience—from seeing, feeling, touching, and realizing that we are, in a way, a *part* of the land from which we live.

The point is that the demands of a farm and the subtle knowledge this work entails require that each person develop certain *virtues*. Being a certain kind of person is necessary for being a farmer at all. It requires patience, care, attentiveness, courage, trust, resignation, persistence, wisdom, intelligence, and a sense of humor. It requires, you might say, that you *fit* your body, and so your character, to the requirements of the land. You might have heard the joke that people and their pets start to look alike. Something similar is true about people and the land. Farmers shape it, and it shapes them. Being *embedded* in the earth changes us.

Gardens, Cultivation, and Vocations

Perhaps it shouldn't surprise us, then, when the Bible says that human beings were originally made to live in a garden (see Genesis 1–2). And our job there was precisely to *cultivate* it. We were made out of the earth originally, and by tending it, we were meant to be continually made out of it.

It's important to note that Genesis says nothing about work being a result of or curse due to sin. The *toil* and *difficulty* of work were increased because of sin (see Genesis 3), but to work the garden was given to us as a *vocation*. In the most literal and bodily terms, that is what human beings are physically made for. The Fathers of the Church sometimes remarked on this calling, noting that, of all the animals of the earth, humans were the only ones without claws or teeth or heavy skins to protect ourselves. We had hands and feet made only for picking fruit and tilling the ground. It's what we were brought out of the ground to do in the first place.

When we were in the garden there was, you might say, an organic unity that existed among humanity, God, and the earth. Humans were made for the earth and the earth for humans, just as they were made for God. In Genesis 1–2, our right relationship to *God* consists of obedience to his command to take care of the earth and subdue it (see Genesis 1:28–30), to tend and keep the garden (see Genesis 2:15), and not to eat of the tree of the knowledge of good and evil (see Genesis 2:17). And we have a right relationship to the *earth*, likewise, by adapting our bodies to their natural fit with creation and by taking up our vocation as its *stewards*. In other words, our relationship with God is inseparable from our relationship with the earth.

It makes sense, then, that the name "human" (in the Bible's Hebrew and in English) is taken from the word for "earth, soil, or ground," so that the name of the first human, "Adam," literally means the "Soil-Man"—or the one who was taken from and made to tend the soil (see Genesis 5:2). Our very name tells us what we are primordially called to do.

Unity of Life through the Land

We can see in Genesis, then, in an embryonic but entirely accurate way, how all of life is included in the God-human-soil relationship. By being connected to the earth, all the different areas of human existence find an organic unity. This is the unity of not only cult and culture but also cultivation. The early American small farmer, the medieval peasant, or today's urban gardener puts her life into her earth. She puts her stamp on it, as Pope St. Leo XIII wrote in *Rerum Novarum*, and her earth puts its stamp on her. She draws her life from it—she eats, drinks, enjoys, creates. Her life and her work are the same; she's an artist, an engineer, and a provider all at once.[2]

From that same earth she raises up a family, which is bound to that same spot in the same ways. She will have to sustain them by feeding them from the same earth. But she will also have to sustain them by teaching them how to sustain themselves by tending and caring for the land. And in so cultivating the land, they develop not just the land but themselves and their community by their intelligence, skill, friendship, prudence, and character. The land yields not just produce but education, tradition, work, art, and culture. The different parts of life arise, one step upon another, all connected integrally with the common task of cultivating the earth.

Each part is necessary and connected with each other part. The physical: for the necessities of life. The moral: for the dispositions needed to do it. Environmental stewardship: to safeguard and protect that land for the next year. Community: because you can't do it alone. Economy: because the resources of life are generated from the earth and from nowhere else. Culture: because traditions have to be passed on and creatively improved upon. Work: because this is the way God gave us to cooperate with him to co-create our lives.

And then finally comes perhaps the most important part: the Church. For most of Western history the Church has been a sort of unofficial preserver of agricultural traditions and practices. It is where all of life is consciously taken up, understood as one whole, especially in relation to God. We see this in the sacramental cycle that moves from Baptism at birth, through First Communion and Confirmation, to marriage (and usually children) or religious life, all the way to anointing and burial at the time of death. Not only have we traditionally had prayers and processions for planting and harvest, for the "churching" of women after childbirth, for birthdays, and so on, but the liturgical seasons themselves often correspond to the agricultural ones: Advent in winter, Lent with sowing and toil, Easter with new life budding forth.

Life experience, scriptural testimony, and the Church's lived tradition all served for most of our history to make blatantly obvious—so obvious that it didn't even really need to be stated—that the agricultural life was a divine vocation. Indeed, in some ways, a life of cultivation was *the* divine vocation.

The Tower of Babel

It should not be surprising, then, that when Adam and Eve eat of the forbidden fruit and transgress that original harmony and get kicked out of the garden, everything goes from bad to worse. Indeed, it's not just the story of the eating of the fruit (see Genesis 3); the whole of the first eleven chapters of the Bible (see Genesis 1–11) form a single Fall narrative that passes through the original sin (see Genesis 3) and the first murder (see Genesis 4), to such general depravity that God sends the flood to kill everybody (see Genesis 6–9), and finally to the Tower of Babel (see Genesis 11).

That tower is clearly meant to symbolize the high point (pun intended) of the way fallen humanity can oppose God's plan for us. In the story, the people of the earth, who still all speak one language, build for *themselves* a city with a "tower with its top in the heavens" to keep themselves, tellingly, from being "scattered abroad upon the face of the whole earth" (Gn 11:4). The Lord then comes down and confuses their language so that they don't succeed in their plan (see Genesis 11:7–9).

The result of their attempt, then, to create an *alternative* human form of life is the opposite of the harmonious union of the Garden of Eden. The Tower of Babel is a story of the peoples of the earth trying to unite *themselves*—but independently of God, and independently of the way they were made to be united.

In place of the divinely given fit between the body and the earth, they use their human ingenuity to try to engineer a way of life in which they don't have to be dependent on the soil any longer. In place of the unity that came about because God had made the earth, other people, and the human body all mutually for one another, they built a tower to rally around and function as their social bond. And, finally and perhaps most strikingly, in place of the garden that was the original human setting, they now live, for the first time, in a *city*. They have broken away from the land and created the first concrete jungle of bricks and mortar (see Genesis 11:2).

The point, of course, is not that scripture is condemning cities in themselves. It's that cities can so many times not only represent, but actually be, the rebellious human attempt to divorce ourselves from (or at least forget about) our irreducible finiteness and dependence on the land.

So for the first time humanity is *scattered* across the face of the earth (see Genesis 11:8). Up to that point, they all had one God-given language (see Genesis 11:1), corresponding to their universally recognized vocation to the land. They spoke "human," as it were—or we might call it "soil-ese." But when they tried to find another source of unity, an alternative corporate human task, God scattered them by giving them different languages. Such fragmentation is simply the natural consequence of their seeking some alternative unity to the one they were given in the garden.[3]

Fragmentation and Life outside the Garden

This bit of biblical history is not a bad prefiguration (I won't call it a prophecy) of what happens when we no longer live anywhere close to our human agricultural vocation as "soil people."

We all enjoy one of the primary fruits of the Industrial Revolution: it makes it physically much easier for most of us to get the necessities of life. All of our mechanical technology has significantly removed the limits, toil, and dependency that come from drawing our life from the soil. But the result of this convenience is that most of us have only the most remote connections with the land.

No one would deny, of course, that our food, shelter, and clothing all come to us *ultimately* from the earth, for there is still no other way to get them. But for most of us this is a theoretical truth, rather than a practical, experiential one. We live at the end of long assembly lines, as it were, that separate our bodies from the sources of their life. When I ask my children, for instance, where their food comes from, their first answer is, "The grocery store." And when we think our food comes from the grocery store, that is a pretty good indication that we have lost something significant about what it is to be human.

Here's the main point in this: by minimizing our connections to the soil, we have also eliminated much of the moral formation, creativity, intelligence, local traditions, natural care for the earth, community life, centrality of the Church—and the unity of all these things—that was built on our links to that soil.

God made us so that our dependence on the land was directly linked to our personal and communal development. The two seem to be inseparable facts of creation. In God's wisdom, the physical limits imposed on humanity by our dependence upon the earth also *developed* our humanity and bound it together.

So, when society begins to move away from an organic connection to the earth, slowly and initially without anyone noticing, the character and unity of life begin to unravel. Now, in our day, for the first time in human history, we can think of life as divided into separate categories such as work, home, community, religion, economy, and morality. These things, for most of society, don't necessarily have anything to do with one another anymore. They are separate compartments of life, each with their own, independent logic.

To be more concrete, before industrialism, labor, home, sex, finances, food, and friends were necessarily bound up together. It was just a fact that sex was related to your ability to produce food, because sex makes children who help you till the earth; finances *were* home-life, because your household made the goods and products that were the basis of the economy; friends made all of this possible, so if you were eating (and hence living), you probably had them. Today, however, these things are no longer necessarily linked. They might *happen* to cross paths, if you go to dinner with friends, or decide to share a bank account with your wife. But they no longer mutually define one another.

Likewise, under these conditions, the retreat of the Church from heart and society was inevitable. Like the other new compartments of modern life, Church now just becomes one *possible* part of it, rather than the beating heart of an indivisible whole. Like children, like what kind of work you do, like whom you have sex with, like who your friends are, like what you eat for supper, the Church under industrialism now becomes one option among many. You can take it or leave it, depending on how it suits your taste, and it accordingly becomes increasingly difficult to see its relevance to "real life." It is no wonder that secularization, as Pope Leo XIII said, was simply part of industrialism itself.[4]

Back to Bubba

Even with just this little bit of background—and there are plenty of things we have not even touched on—we can hopefully appreciate why the Industrial Revolution was so revolutionary. With the possible exception of the advent of Christianity, it is hard to imagine a more total set of changes in society happening within so relatively few years. Like the early Christian revolution, it really has turned the whole "world upside down" (Acts 17:6).

And we can also glimpse a little more clearly how insightful Bubba was. For when people criticized him for not getting a job, they were implicitly asking him to live more fully in the fragmented nature of industrial life. As it was, even though he wasn't a farmer, by simply staying outside of the conventional social world he had managed to avoid much of that fragmentation. He did his work with his friends, often sharing the panhandling proceeds; he lived where he worked, with those same friends; they ate together, laughed together, and entertained one another.

But the critics wanted him to break up his life the way that they broke up theirs. They wanted him to have work *and* friends *and* a home *and* food, and so on—all separate from one another. But Bubba intuited that was a raw deal, and he said no.

In the next two chapters we'll see what we can do about this fragmentation in our own lives too. Building on what we've explored here, we'll look in more depth at our vocation to good work, how we pursued this in Durham, and the little revolution that took place in Bubba's life when, a few years later, he traded his tent for a farmhouse.

9

A PHILOSOPHY OF LABOR

People today seem to be increasingly dissatisfied with their jobs. Not only is it the case that in society at large the turnover rate is higher than it has ever been and the service industry is perpetually short-staffed, but there's also a certain amount of conscious popular reflection about what we spend our days doing. Some evidence is the fact that a recent book about work, *Shop Class as Soulcraft: An Inquiry into the Value of Work*, recently reached the *New York Times* best-seller list.

The good news is that even in the ordinary circles of Catholics my family runs in, folks are taking measures to enrich their work experience. Rob, a thirty-eight-year-old father of four, looking to get out of the model-home contractor business, recently took some evening classes in the trade of timber-framing. Brian, a thirty-five-year-old father of four, an engineer for Best Buy, and an ex-military nuclear submarine designer, has started a side-business that connects the produce of Catholic farmers in outstate Minnesota with Catholic customers in the Twin Cities. Several active members of a local parish—including my friends Megan and Nate—all with jobs within the mainstream economy, have started a weekend pop-up market that sells roasted coffee, ceramics, paintings, and other items they've made themselves at home.

None of these people, that I know of, has read up on Peter Maurin's philosophy of work, or anyone else's. They also run in different circles and go to different parishes, and so it appears they've come to their resolutions independently. What they all do have in common is a sense, a gut feeling, that their usual nine-to-five is somehow not cutting it for them. They all have started integrating work that is more tangible, physical, or tactile into their lives. And they are doing it because, as someone recently put it to me, "It just feels good." They've intuited that work is important and that they want something more out of it than a paycheck. And they have all gone about addressing that desire in creative and beautiful ways—little ways.

In this chapter, we're going to take a closer look at some of the more specific things the Catholic tradition has to say about work. This will help us see what's behind that common gut feeling—why this kind of work feels good. We'll parse out "good" work from "less good" work and see that most of the time what we commonly mean by work is actually labor stripped of what makes it good. But this will also involve us seeing what makes work such an invaluable divine gift, as well as what we can do to transform our own experience of it.

As we explore these ideas, it's important to keep the examples of Rob, Brian, and the rest in mind. I mention them in part because they show what it can look like practically to grapple with work as a divine vocation. It's not out of reach or irresponsible; families with kids can do it, and more and more Catholics are starting to feel this tug every day.[1]

So, after we set out Peter's philosophy of labor here (which, as we'll see, is really just the Church's philosophy of labor as articulated by a number of popes), the next chapter will be almost entirely devoted to the manner in which this new way of looking at things materialized for us in Durham and literally transformed our community. So if Rob and Brian pique your curiosity, there are more examples on the way.

A Different Kind of Poverty

In the last chapter, we saw what a relatively new thing modern industrial life is. For us in Durham, this was an important realization, and we wanted to go deeper. So, in addition to the social encyclicals, we also started exploring Peter Maurin's list of great books—writers he had learned from and recommended to others. These included, among others, Catholic agrarian thinkers such as G. K. Chesterton, Hilaire Belloc, and Vincent McNabb. We also read more contemporary authors such as Wendell Berry and Ivan Illich. These folks helped us clarify and make practical the basic insights we had gleaned so far regarding industrial life.

One of the first things that became apparent was that the poverty we were encountering every day was a particularly *modern* poverty. There have always been poor people. Most people throughout history have been poor, and sometimes very poor. But, as we saw in the last chapter, until recently the poor have also had at their disposal the means of producing a living for themselves and the knowledge required to do it. This gave the poor a significant measure of independence, for they could take care of themselves. It also gave them dignity, for they were still creative, resourceful, and very much their own bosses. It was feasible to have very little income, and yet be quite well off.

Poverty today is very different. In our economy you can't get by without a regular flow of *money,* and that's because just about all the necessities of life today, besides air and water, are commodities. That is, as opposed to making things for the household and the local community to consume, we make things almost exclusively to be bought or sold on the market. So to get money—the lifeblood of our world—the Guys on the Hill were utterly *dependent* upon begging, state or institutional handouts, or wage labor.

This is poverty of a brand-new kind. To single it out, Dorothy called it *destitution*, because it's poverty without any recourse. Perhaps worst of all, because it's poverty without independence, it's also largely poverty without any dignity. And yet we have more of it today than ever before, and in growing numbers.

This, it's worth noting, is the problem with the common argument that industrialism has raised the standard of living across the world even for the poorest. It's true that even the poorest now *consume more commodities* than ever before, but at the cost of being utterly dependent upon those commodities, their creators, and a cash income.

The Standard Question

All of this led to the issue of work for us, because the most obvious thing about poor or homeless people these days is that "they don't have enough money." And so the obvious standard question—the question we heard over and over again from folks interested in or curious about the hospitality house—was, "So do you try to help them get jobs?"

The answer was that we hadn't really thought about it very much. We weren't opposed to the Guys looking for jobs, but it also wasn't something we actively pushed on anyone. But the frequency with which people wanted to know about it showed us that there are some deeply rooted feelings about work in our culture. The unstated assumption often appeared to be that if we weren't helping them find jobs, we were somehow being irresponsible. And underneath *that* assumption seemed to be the feeling—often vague and unformed—that anyone who is actively working for a living is in some sense morally better than someone who is not.

We wanted to dig around and underneath these assumptions a little bit, with the suspicion that understanding them better would help us see our relationship with the Guys more clearly. And this is where we got into what Peter had learned from the popes.

Good Work

We tend to define work as any activity at all that you get paid for. This is what people mean when they ask if we help them get jobs. In fact, the presumption can be that the longer the hours, the more menial the tasks, and the lower the wages, the *more* this really shows someone's character. Because part of the mark of a good person is that he or she is "willing to work."

Yet this, we quickly learned, is a modern, and not a Catholic, definition of work.

In the first place, no Catholic *really* thinks that just any activity that comes with a wage is honorable. Prostitution, child labor, and abortions fit that description, but we would want to say not only that each of those employments produces bad results but also that they are bad for those who do them. Those are examples of bad work.

The question is, then, What makes work good? What makes it part of our divine vocation?

We can begin by taking a look at a statement by Pope Leo XIII about the intimate connection that should exist between the worker and what he produces : *Rerum Novarum*. He writes that when man "turns the activity of his mind and the strength of his body toward procuring the fruits of nature, by such an act he makes his own that portion of nature's field which he cultivates—*that portion on which he leaves, as it were, the impress of his personality.*"[2] To place the impress or stamp of our personality on something—that is the first characteristic of good work. There are a couple of different aspects of this that are worth noting.

First, in impressing himself on nature, the worker takes the lower parts of creation—wood, metal, dirt, or whatever—and he, so to speak, makes it a part of *human* life. It is not just lying out there as part of the irrational creation anymore; it now takes a rational place in the order of your life. When Rob puts his timber frames together, he has raised up the irrational order into the rational order.

Second, this work makes its object *personal*—it puts not just any stamp, but *your* stamp on it. That field that you sow, that table that you build, that motorcycle that you put together has something of *you* in it. So, by working and stamping things with your "you-ness," you are, as St. John Paul II said, enacting your divine vocation to be a creator, a little bit in the same way that God is Creator.[3] That's one of the reasons why Megan's pottery is so beautiful—there's a good bit of *her* in it.

But there's even more. For in stamping our image on things, because *we* are made in *God's* image, we are also stamping *his* image on things. Good work, then, raises up the material creation not only into the human realm, but into the divine realm. Only humans, of all that God made, have his image and likeness (see Genesis 1:26–27); the rest of the world does not, even though God declared it was *good*. Yet *we* can put God's image and likeness on the rest of creation, when we put our own stamp on it.

And this image-bearing potential, Leo says, is where *property* comes from. For by stamping his personality on the world, the worker "makes his own that portion of nature's field which he cultivates." "Property" is just a common word that means "one's own." It is *your own*, then, because it has your own *image and likeness* on it. This view of property stands in contrast to that of some influential Enlightenment philosophers, who thought that one can use or abuse property as one pleases because it is a rational, objective matter of rights.

The meal that you prepared and set out, or the garden that you dug, planted, and weeded—and the way each looks so good in its symmetry, colors, and how the light catches it—is "yours" in the best sense of the term. What you made is like you, and the pride we take in this kind of property is a good kind of pride because we made these things, we see ourselves in them, and we also see the divine image *through* what we have made. If we know Rob or Megan, and then we see their work, we can affirm that *this* house or *this* cup really is *theirs* in a way that is not true for houses or cups that are mass-produced.

Leo adds one more important point in *Rerum Novarum*. He says that "the results of labor should belong to those who have bestowed their labor" and this for "the preservation of life, and for life's well-being."[4] In other words, another measure of *good* work is that what it produces is consumed by those who produce it. There should exist, we might say, a personal connection between the laborer and the fruits of his labor. Good work is growing food to eat it, making chairs to sit on them, chopping wood for your fireplace, fixing your car to drive it.

Leo gives us several criteria, then, for evaluating the work that we do. Work should (1) put our stamp on the world and (2) create property, and (3) the property, as well as the fruits of the property, should contribute to the life and well-being of the worker. Or, to sum it up, the worker should own the means of production and make his living off of them.

This helps explain why work of this kind—like Rob's timber framing or Megan's pottery—feels so good. We have an intrinsic interest in it, because *we* are going to use what comes out of it; and while we work, we are looking forward to being proud of something that shows what we are and what we can do. It's engaging work; it holds our attention; we delight in it.

And all of this, finally, as St. John Paul II emphasized so well, is meant to make us holy. That's the ultimate reason for work—why it's a divine calling. This is not one *additional* criterion, but the goal of the other criteria. All work should be ordered toward making us and society better people and better Catholics. It should serve the common good. Leo's criteria are so important precisely because they serve as guides for what kind of work accomplishes these goals.

Not-So-Good Work

But clearly not all work meets Leo's criteria. I mentioned above Bubba's aversion to working at the gas station, and we noted in general that much of the work available both to him and in Peter's time was below human dignity. We're now in a position to see why.

A job at the gas station isn't demoralizing just because it's boring and hard on your legs. It is also demoralizing because it doesn't meet any of the criteria of good work Leo articulated. And the same is true for just about every other job our unemployed friends around St. Joseph's could imagine getting, whether it "produces" anything or not: waiting tables, loading boxes at UPS, canning tuna, or refining oil.

Let's go through Pope Leo's criteria in relation to these kinds of jobs. First, such work doesn't put one's stamp on anything; at most it puts a machine's stamp on something. This means that the work is not personal in any way, but predetermined by set categories to be as efficient as possible.

Nor does it produce any property of one's own. One receives a wage precisely to make property for someone else. It is the very point of your job that you don't end up with anything directly connected with what you've been doing all day. A wage is only connected with it *indirectly*. If you make cans of tuna, you don't take any of them home; you get money that you can use to go to the store to *buy* tuna.

Nor do you produce anything with which you directly provide for your needs. These jobs break the natural cycle of giving your body to the natural materials of the earth and those materials, in turn, nourishing your body.

That is, we are alienated or separated from the fruits of our labor. They are taken away from us, and we have only money to show for it at the end of the day. Unlike the farmer or craftsman, we are not surrounded by things that our own hands have made. Our body is separated from what we have and what we consume, for what we have and what we consume did not come from our own bodies.

I still remember going to my grandparents' house as a child and being told where just about everything in their house came from and who had made it and when. They were surrounded by the fruits of their and their community's labor. It was a deeply *personal* material existence, and that was because their *labor* was personal. They took joy in work, because they were making their life. Their work was their life and their life was their work; and people were proud of it.

Most modern work, especially those jobs the poor are likely to get, is very different. Our lives now *begin* where our work *ends*. In order to live we have to sell our labor. Our work, our divine vocation, is no longer our life, and it has become a commodity in the service of making other commodities. We sell our life vocation—our work—because in an industrial world it's the only way we have to continue to get what we need to continue to exist.

We don't work, in other words, because it's part of living well. We don't think of it as part of how a human flourishes as a human. We work in order *to simply exist*—to make money to sustain our bodily needs. And so our work is separated from what we call "life." The time we spend doing labor is a *sacrifice* of life for the sake of what we call "real life." Real life begins for us when we go home, or to the bar, or to the soccer field. That's what we're really here for. What we've been doing all day is something else.

Degrading Work

It should not be surprising that, under these conditions, work can become not only not-so-good because of the toll it takes on our bodies, but degrading because it lacks those things that make it good for our souls. This destitution is what Peter was especially concerned about. Helping people get jobs, therefore, might not really be *helping* them at all.

Because of the extreme pressure of competition in a consumer society, tasks are divided in order to make work more efficient. We have all heard of this division of labor, and it has always existed in all societies. But our division is so extreme that it often simplifies tasks so much that there is little room for our own creativity and input. This is especially the case the more mechanized and computerized the work is. The *human* element is increasingly eliminated, and the more this happens, the more we are doing the work of animals. In farmwork, animals need humans to drive them, because they are not themselves creative and intelligent. The more the lead in labor is taken by routines, programs, and minute bureaucratic regulations, the more we do jobs that, as we say, a monkey could do.

This is degrading because it doesn't develop our virtues and make us holy as work is supposed to. It is a general truth of the spiritual life that if we're not moving forward, we don't just stay stationary—we slide backwards. And if we're not moving forward toward holiness in our work—for eight hours or more a day—we don't develop those virtues of creativity, care, patience, courage, attentiveness, and all the others we noted in the last chapter. In fact, we can even slide into their opposite vices. So it's no wonder that Pope Leo associated industrial labor with "the prevailing moral degeneracy"[5] in *Rerum Novarum*. If we do the work of monkeys, we become more like them.

I think what Bubba might have really been offended at was the suggestion that he should do the work of an animal. Rob, Brian, and the others, too, have found things more worthy of their own divine calling.

The Common Good?

But there is one more important criterion for good work that Leo mentions in *Rerum Novarum*: it should serve the common good.[6] We don't need to go into any detailed definition of the common good to see one major way that most of our jobs fall short of it.

The industrial economy is premised, as we mentioned in a different connection above, on always producing the next new thing. This means—and this point is so important that it's worth underlining here—that we live in the midst of a sort of perpetual cultural revolution.

New things are what sell. So, for a time at least, when you have the next new invention—the best phone so far, or the best

nail gun, or the best machine gun—everybody is going to buy
your product. But if you don't innovate, you're left behind and
will soon be out of business because everybody is going to buy
the new, more advanced, "better" thing your competitors are
selling. Making money in our economy *demands* that the old
get left behind as quickly as possible and that something new
take its place.

This means that the consumer economy is always shifting. It
will always be preying on traditional communities and old-fashioned ways of doing things. If you feel like the world is changing every minute and you can never set your feet on anything
solid, this drive for innovation and novelty is one big reason why.
As Leo himself implied in *Rerum Novarum*, there is nothing at
all *conservative* about the industrial economy.[7] If the Industrial
Revolution is the one really revolutionary revolution, that's in
part because it has *never stopped* turning society upside down.
It wasn't just a historical moment in the nineteenth century; it
is still going on.

Most of the work available today, then, dependent as it is on
this sort of creative destruction, fails the criterion of the common good. It does so not so much by producing things that are
evil, though it does that as well. It does so by creating a society
that is so transitory that the very notion of the common good
becomes difficult to imagine.

Stability, continuity across time, shared traditions, and a
common history of a unified way of ordering life—these are
prerequisites for the pursuit of the common good. In a society
like ours, these things are largely absent, and so we just have
one different form of life following another. How can we build
something *common* if each new generation cannot imagine what
life was like when their parents were children? Unfortunately,
most modern work only contributes to this perpetual revolution.

The Little Way versus the Perpetual Revolution

All of this can sound like an overwhelming bummer. And, in a way, it is. Most modern work is work stripped of the things that make it good. It doesn't fall into the category of overtly sinful behavior, like the work of the prostitute or the abortionist, but it also is far from what work should be. That's not good news. But it's also not the end of the story.

Part of the gift of the Catholic Worker's sharp critique of society is to help us see our world for what it is—for what the Church has told us it is. Dorothy and Peter refuse to let us put our heads in the sand and pretend the status quo is anywhere near the Gospel's ideals. It is not. The Church wants us to look reality squarely in the face. And this is good because we want to live as much *in* reality as we can.

At the same time, when it comes to not-so-good work, the Church takes a pragmatic and pastoral approach. As much as Pope Leo critiques modern work, he also clearly understands that, in the world as it is, many people will have to continue to take the not-so-good jobs that are available, and that you can't blame them for making that decision.[8] Dorothy and Peter always echoed this, while continuing to issue the summons to work as a divine vocation. They had no judgment for the jobs we have in the meantime—and perhaps indefinitely.

This pragmatic approach was ultimately the solution we came to regarding the Guys. If somebody wanted help with an application or a ride to an interview—no problem. But we also didn't actively press the matter.

For us, however, this was no longer just a question of the Guys' work. The more we thought about it—the more *I* thought about it—the more it became apparent that the issue involved me as well. At the time I was teaching as an adjunct professor at a few area universities. While that work was good in some respects, I increasingly saw that it still basically failed all Leo's criteria, and that the university put my own work to the service of creating a society in which, as a Christian, I felt ever more out of place.

I wanted good work. *I* wanted to get my hands dirty with tasks that would engage my whole body in a way I could touch, feel, smell, and maybe eventually taste.

And so once again I found Thérèse's little way so important.

It'd be easy to feel as if extending the Gospel to all of our lives—much less just finding some good work—is going to be close to impossible, given all the ways the world is stacked against us. It can just seem like a very bad time to be a Christian. But Thérèse makes exactly the opposite point through her little way. As it was for the early Christians, *of course* the world is against us, but it is precisely our task to engage it, love it, and bring it healing—one person, one little-way action at a time—*while* it does its best to oppose us. That's just how Christianity works.

Like Rob and Brian, we don't have to wait till we have a Christian society before we can get on with actually being Christians or finding work that "just feels good." We have everything we need right now. The Lord has put us here exactly for this reason: to be little-way Christians in the face of the perpetual revolution. What will come of our efforts is not up to us. We don't have to plan the course to a Christian society beforehand. We just have to start. And the good news is that every little step toward a life of good work is itself good work.

The little way is a reminder that it is a very *good* time to be a Christian.

10

GARDENS, CHICKENS, AND DUMPSTERS

After a couple of years at the Maurin House, some of our core members branched off and rented houses a few blocks away. They provided additional hospitality to the homeless, and each hosted a weekly dinner. The Maurin House remained the main house, not least because it was where the chapel was, which we continued to see as the center of our life together. We named these houses the Thérèse House (for the saint of the little way) and the Elizabeth House (for St. Elizabeth of Hungary), and they allowed us to continue to experiment with putting into practice the ideas we were discussing about work.

Our friend Luke had just moved back in to town from Georgia and was taking on a leading role in the Elizabeth House. That property had a little side yard—surely less than a tenth of an acre, but big enough for a decent-sized garden. This was to be our first try at what we came to call "shortening the supply chain," by which we meant our little-way attempts to reduce the distance between ourselves and the earth.

And so a garden seemed an obvious place to start. We were certainly not going to get rid of the supply chains, but there were lots of little-way things we could do to shorten them, which we came to see was the same thing as putting good work back into our lives, one step at a time. Every link we could take out of that chain was one thing that we were doing to put our stamp on the world.

Only a few of us (not me) had the faintest notion of what to plant, how and when to plant it, and how to keep it alive. Gardening sounds simple enough, but its complexity soon revealed to me how utterly practical this reconnection with the soil was going to be, and that I had absolutely no idea what I was doing.

Thankfully, Luke knew a little, and a neighboring Protestant community had some members who had grown up on a farm. So we dug up that side yard and put in some tomatoes, sweet peppers, jalapenos, summer squash, cucumbers, lettuce, and of course sweet potatoes since we were in North Carolina.

Gardening is pretty common, even if less so today than in the past. But I was a beginner. What impressed me so much was the visceral, physical experience of these first halting steps. It was as if I had discovered my body, and specifically, my *senses,* for the first time. The smell of the dirt, the sound of the bugs, the feel of the shovel when it hit a rock, and the soreness of my muscles the day after digging—nothing that I had done as a teenager in suburbia or as a bookworm in a university had engaged the whole of me in the same way. I started to see that this kind of work really does "just feel good."

Like meeting Christ in the poor, our garden opened for me a path to God that that I never knew existed, but that had been there all the time. I was discovering that there was more to my humanity than I had imagined. It was exhilarating. I started to understand firsthand how it could be that peasants, farmers, artisans, and craftsmen throughout history could not only endure but thrive in such work. It was work that could be grueling and frustrating, but it was also deeply pleasurable, almost sensual. There was real satisfaction in it.

But Luke wasn't done. He also had designs on a small flock of chickens. Someone in the area had a big, old coop for sale for $100. And so one Saturday afternoon we rented a U-Haul, picked it up, and got it set up beside the garden. A couple of weeks later we picked up the birds from a friend who was getting rid of hers, put them in the trunk of the car (have you ever tried to get eight scared chickens to stay in a trunk long enough to shut the lid?), and moved them in.

Chickens are goofy animals that are cheap to buy and easy to care for. Even I learned to do so with relative ease. But I was unprepared for the way they brought out the natural, self-sustaining unity in our tiny little human-garden-chicken setup. We fed the chickens feed from the store, but we also gave them table scraps. They, of course, gave us eggs—delicious, wonderful eggs that, to my surprise, were much more flavorful than the ones I was used to from the store.

But they also gave us poop. We took their hay-poop mixture and added it to the compost heap we had started when we dug up the yard. We also composted table scraps the chickens didn't want, like banana peels and their own egg shells. Soon I was eating veggies made with compost, which was made from chicken poop and eggshells, which were made from scraps from my table. And some of those scraps, as time went on, went directly to the chickens, which made poop for compost and eggs for eating and so on. I thought all this was so cool!

Of course, these are the most basic ecological connections, which many readers may justifiably laugh at. *Of course* that's what happens. And, of course, somewhere in my head I knew, theoretically, that that's how the world could work. But all my experience was of a different reality—the one that most of us live with every day: eggs come from the store; their packages, shells, and any scraps go in the trash and get carted off somewhere else.

My household had never consumed anything that I produced; it had only ever consumed things made by somebody else. The circle of life was somewhere "out there." Bringing it close to home (literally) and putting *myself* in the middle of it—putting my stamp on it by means of my work—was another remarkable experience I was not expecting. For the first time in my life, I was *participating* in creation the way that it was meant to be. We had shortened just a few simple supply chains, and I felt, even with just these steps, more human—more like a "Soil-Man"—than before.

We, of course, didn't grow and produce anywhere near enough to sustain ourselves. But we wondered if there were others around who did, and if we could get more of our food from them. And so naturally we turned our eyes to the local farmer's market that met every Saturday morning. Here were many people who, for a variety of different reasons, lived much more profoundly within the rhythm of God's creation than we could ever dream of. Most of them were not industrial farmers and were committed to local living and shortening the supply chains themselves. It only made sense that we could shorten the supply chains by supporting these folks as much as we could.

We also started being intentional about cooking our own meals. Making food from scratch, or at least buying some of the ingredients and putting them together ourselves, got us just a little closer to the earth by removing the processing of prepared foods by factories and industrial kitchens.

Finding good food and cooking it together became a regular activity. It's also a great way to build community. Instead of spending a couple of hours watching a movie on a Saturday afternoon and then going out to eat, we'd walk to the farmer's market together and then prepare a meal. It's something to do together, it's good work, and it shortens a few supply chains.

Then one day we were leaving prayer and we noticed something interesting. St. Joseph's lies adjacent to a Whole Foods grocery store, with the back of the store facing the church. One of the employees was loading a whole trash can full of perfectly good watermelon halves into one of the dumpsters. Luke ran over.

"Hey, are you just throwing those away?"

"Yeah, they're about to expire tomorrow," the gal said. "But there's nothing wrong with them."

"Can we take them?" Luke asked.

"I can't give them to you," she said, "but if you were to take them when I wasn't out here, there'd be nothing I could do about that."

And so began our habit of checking the dumpster every day. The employee gave us some insider info about when the "expiring" food came out and when it would get picked up so we could time it as best we could.

On the one hand, this was kind of cool because, well, we were poor graduate students and it was free food that helped supplement our dinners. On the other hand, we realized, this was another way of shortening the supply lines. Our industrial food system produces an incredible amount of waste. Much of it is not reintegrated into God's waste-and-renewal cycle like the one we had discovered in our side yard. A lot of it is thrown away in its noncompostable packaging to sit in a landfill somewhere.

So not only could we get some free food (always welcome), but we could take the food out of the industrial cycle and repurpose it to the use of our own bodies, chickens, and gardens. This also meant that we didn't have to buy that food from the store, which would be perpetuating the habits that produced all this waste in the first place.

All this was, of course, just a drop in the ocean. But once again it wasn't the scale of the thing we were concerned about.

We weren't doing this primarily to "make a difference." We wanted to do what we could to be faithful to the place and time where God had placed us. The rescue of that food, which God had made, after all, was a good action in itself. It was our own symbolic way of hoeing a row or milking a cow. It was a nod to the truth about human beings that we found in Genesis, but also felt in our bones. It made a difference to *us*.

And dumpster diving, it turned out, could be entertaining, even hilarious (if somewhat gross) good work. Often we had to have someone on the lookout for the manager while another one of us literally got into the dumpster (hence dumpster *diving*) to pull out the good stuff, often from among not-so-good stuff. It was a sort of stinky sting operation. At one point, this involved a secret signal (like a birdcall, I believe) in case the manager was coming. It also sometimes meant that one or more of us made the church smell like something other than incense and varnished pews at evening prayer. And then there was real work still left to be done: we had to haul the produce up to the house, pick over any rotten parts, and so on. All this bound us together more closely. Luke had found us another little bit of good work.

Bubba on the Farm

It is perhaps unsurprising that after living with our gardens and chickens for a couple of years, the more adventurous among us started seriously talking about what it would be like to add a small farm to our community. The original Catholic Worker house, founded by Day and Maurin in New York City, had done it, so why couldn't we?

Eventually we connected with a woman at a local church who ran a small farm about an hour away from Durham. She mostly sold her produce to local residents who signed up to receive a box each week in a scheme commonly known as Community Supported Agriculture (CSA). She was struggling to do all the work herself, and she also had a large farmhouse that was not being used. She offered to have some of us move to the house, help her out with the work, and have some share in the produce as well as the use of some land.

Two core families decided to go for it. By this time there had been a couple of marriages in the community, as well as a few children born. Life on the land especially appealed to them. There were places for children to run; real, good work for them to do; real things to learn; and plenty of space to grow into.

And, as it turned out, three of the Guys wanted to go as well—and one of them was Bubba.

Bubba's life in Durham was not atypical for the Guys. He was friendly and fun to be around, as I've mentioned, but he also had his own ways of dealing with the stresses of life.

Up at St. Joe's his usual mode when nothing else was going on was to sit on an old paint bucket off by himself under a large tree, put his headphones on, put his head between his hands and his elbows on his knees, drink a lot of Old English, and remain like that—for hours. I always took it as a totally understandable, if somewhat sad, mode of distraction in the midst of the concrete, noise, and heat of a big city that more or less tried to act like he and all the other Guys didn't exist. I'm sure it was also his way of dealing with his own demons, whatever they might be.

Yet it was clear, after they had been on the farm for a while, that there Bubba had found an entirely new rhythm. None of the Guys were required to work—they were simply given hospitality at the farm just like they were in Durham. But Bubba had clearly found that he *wanted* to work. Every day, he—and often the other Guys as well—went off to the fields and helped plant, weed, harvest, move bags of rocks, spread compost, dig, chop, or fell trees.

Bubba's own job was to take care of the farm's large flock of chickens. He'd tend the water and food day and night, collect the eggs, and clean the coop, and he was especially good at showing the birds off when different groups would come out for farm tours.

"Look at that one," he'd say, pointing to the rooster. "You'd strut around like that too if it was just you and all them ladies. That's the man of the house right there."

And I can't help mentioning the good-natured banter and joshing between the Guys while they worked. There's nothing better to pass the time on a hot North Carolina morning than listening to three old friends jaw at one another. It was funnier comedy than any movie you've seen—as long as you don't mind sentences composed primarily of four-letter words.

Another one of Bubba's jobs was to harvest veggies each evening for dinner. He also had to teach us how to cook some of them: kids from the Midwest don't know what to do with okra, and to this day I still think it's slimy and slightly gross. But Bubba fried it up some old Southern way so that the North Carolinians loved it, and the Northerners found it at least (almost) edible.

Not right away, then, but over time, you could see the change all this brought about in Bubba. He lost some weight, he drank much less, and, in general, he seemed to have more of a purpose in life. "He just came alive," one of the community members told me.

That was my impression, too, when we would go down to visit. And Bubba had already been pretty alive! Getting close to the land had clearly tapped into something in him—it was as if he was made for it.

Keeping the Connections: A Catholic Whole

These were some of our little-way attempts to shorten the supply lines and so tap in just a little more to our divine vocation. But it can be easy, reading what I have just written, to lose the deep connection between this lifestyle and the main themes of this book. What does all of this have to do with building thick Catholic communities, common prayer, life with the poor, the Gospel as social fabric, and so on? Had we just drifted into liberal, hippie "food justice"?

I want to end this chapter by pulling all of these threads together, so that we keep a properly *Catholic* understanding of the connection with the land. For Pope Leo and Peter Maurin would want to argue that shortening the supply lines, which is the same as finding good work, is not just one particular possible way of being Catholic among other options. The land is not just one "issue" that our community happened to be particularly passionate about, any more than we had a "special calling" or "particular ministry" to the poor or to build community. Rather, these are *ordinary* things we are all called to do just because we are ordinary Catholics. And they all go together.

Keeping the Connections: Community

First, then, the kind of work we've described in this chapter is part of those social bonds that any healthy Catholic community needs. As much as we may like one another, real community cannot just be a matter of hanging out. It is always a product of having shared *tasks*, as we have seen throughout the book in various ways. And for Christian community, that means shared Gospel tasks. So, to the shared work of prayer, breakfast, and hospitality, we now added the care of gardens, chickens, and dumpsters.

For one thing, this strengthened our social bonds simply by our having to regularly coordinate and plan together. Who was going to water and weed, feed the chickens, turn the compost, and when? And what about when someone is sick? Or out of town?

Then there was the work itself. Not only did we now have a little bit of good work; we had good *community* work. And community work is especially important because it forms relationships between people who might not otherwise have much in common. Sitting and staring at each other over a cup of coffee, Monty and I would quickly run out of things to talk about. But now we had the garden, the coop, or the dumpster in common. Our *being with* each other was now based on a mutual *being for*. It didn't matter if we abstractly liked each other, because we both were committed to the garden project (think back to the projects we talked about in chapter 3), and so we were committed to each other. I sometimes think there is so much social anxiety today in part because we have so few of these very practical relationships.

Keeping the Connections: The Poor

But this kind of communal good work is also directly connected to hospitality to the poor. Pope Leo's teaching, as we've seen, is that today's new kind of poverty is caused by industrialism, a system that has left much of the population, he says in *Rerum Novarum*, under a yoke "not much better than slavery itself."[1] As we saw, Leo argued that modern poverty is historically novel because the poor today no longer have recourse to any productive property that formerly gave them a measure of independence. The implication of this is that the homelessness that we were living with in the hospitality house day by day was, according to Leo, directly linked to our separation from the land and to our lack of good work.

It's unsurprising then that Leo suggested that the remedy for this situation was a reconnection with the land. If as a society we could start moving toward investing in property that we could live from, we could all start to develop more independence, and the general welfare would increase.[2] Accordingly, to Peter's way of thinking, the more we could all inch toward the land right now, the less modern poverty there would be. Hospitality houses and good work are not only nourishment for our souls; they are also twin Christian solutions to the same social problem. We do them out of devotion—to find God in the poor and in the land—but their effects also redound to the good of society.

So, in spite of its dreamy or idealistic associations, getting back to the land in little ways is actually the Catholic Worker's most *practical* component. It's dealing directly with a major social problem. We can contrast this with what are often thought of as the hard-nosed, "realistic" solutions to poverty: government programs or new theories of social organization or better economic regulations and so on. There's no doubt that such strategies are probably often necessary in the short term to alleviate some of the suffering of the poor. But insofar as they never question the *industrial* nature of our society, they are not actually addressing the cause of our malaise. Leo is encouraging us to go to the root of things.

Keeping the Connections: Personal Commitments

But by far our biggest motivator to shorten the supply chain was simply the friendships and commitments we had made. It was personal.

I loved *my* community—this particular one, with *these* friends, Tyler, Crystal, Justin, Mallory—and *our* peculiar rhythms. I loved it, and it had become a big part of who I was. We've seen many ways that being closer to the land is good for community and many ways that our dominant culture is bad for community. I saw this analysis play out in very concrete terms.

For I started to see that to opt for Tyler and Crystal, Justin and Mallory, was also to opt for our garden, our chickens, and our dumpsters. The habits of attentive care for our little plot of earth, and the little ways we could express our commitments to shortening the supply chains, were the same habits that resisted fragmentation. On the other hand, the more we gave in to the convenience of big stores, smartphones, text messages, social media, fast food, and supermarkets, the less we would need one another and the easier it would be for each of us to walk away and do our own thing. Loving my community meant setting myself against this, and setting myself against this meant shortening the supply lines.

It was similarly personal with the poor. I saw Christ in *these* Guys—Crete, Danny, Mac—and had real relationships with them. How could I knowingly support the forces that made life so hard for them? How could I not support local farmers whose work established little oases like the one where Bubba was thriving? How could I shop at the mega-mart down the road that every day competed to put Bubba's farm out of business?

Finally, it's worth remembering that all of this had started with the liturgy. I had started praying at St. Joe's because I knew that prayer was absolutely essential to our relationship with God; it's how we commune with him. But, as we saw in Genesis, this relationship is always a part of a broader relationship and vocation to the earth. Our relationship with God comes in part *through* our relationship with the earth.

And there is perhaps no community more Catholic, and more committed to liturgy *and* land as part of being Catholic, than the Benedictines. Their motto, *Ora et labora*—which means

"Prayer and work"—often appeared in large letters across the pages of the *Catholic Worker*.

By *ora*, the Benedictines mean the Church's liturgy, which is their primary work. But they have also usually been farmers, and so for them *labora* in the field is also a form of prayer—a simple continuation of the *labora* they do in the chapel. And to this day they embody this connection by literally praying while they work. And so they have the prayer in the chapel that is work, and the work in the field that is prayer.

Their point, of course, is that all of their life becomes one liturgy, one continuous work of God. Cult and cultivation, just like in Genesis, are inseparable from one another. Shortening the supply chain, then, if the monks have anything to say about it, is just a little participation in the liturgy itself. It doesn't get more Catholic than that.

This combination of prayer and work, cult and cultivation, again, made it personal. We talked before about how it ought not to surprise us if we feel distant from God but we have not sought him in one of the major places he promises he'll show up: the face of the poor. The same is true with our vocation to the earth: sometimes the best thing I can do for my prayer life is to get my hands dirty. It's what they were made for.

11

VOLUNTARY POVERTY

One of the most striking things about Catholic Worker communities is often their voluntary poverty: many times one finds in these communities ordinary, respectable, educated Americans who have, in various degrees, given up their possessions in favor of a life of material want. Voluntary poverty was an essential piece of Dorothy and Peter's message, and I think it is an essential part of remaking Catholic community today. What do we mean by it? A few examples will give us a general idea.

My friend Tony, mentioned in a previous chapter, was a single guy. He once had a life of wealth, comfort, and indulgence, but found it dissatisfying. Now he pursues what he often refers to as "a simple life." Since I have known him, he usually rents a single bedroom in someone else's house, stays for long periods of time with friends, or house sits. He works part-time at a dance studio doing administration and makes enough for rent, groceries, coffee, and smokes. He spends the rest of his time either at St. Joe's, at the Maurin House, or in the coffee shops on the main drag of Durham, trying to build community among the poor, the merchants, and the customers. He could have made lots of money, but he chose poverty instead.

Another example: The Cross family lives in North Minneapolis. John works as a pastoral associate at a large Catholic parish.

His wife, Mary, stays home with their four children. John's job pays well for a church job (we could estimate about $60,000 a year for our purposes), but with their family size they still qualify for food stamps.

Wanting to share life with people who live in a poor part of town, they managed to afford a foreclosure in a historically lower-class neighborhood. They finished the basement and offer hospitality there, usually to long-term guests they get to know from the streets and who become, as it were, a part of the family. They are well-known on the block, and they get lots of knocks on the door from folks looking for a ride or a few bucks or someone to talk to. Their community, and in a way their family, is possible because they are voluntarily poor.

A third example: Back when the Durham community was just beginning to form, Mallory and Justin were the first married couple to move into the hospitality house. Justin was in graduate school at Duke, and Mallory was the breadwinner who worked at a large financial consulting firm in downtown Raleigh in a very well-paying gig.

Then one day she announced that she was going to quit. The job took too much time, it was not very good work, and she wanted to spend more of her days around the house. She took a part-time job at a secondhand clothing store close by in Durham. She had decided, as Justin put it, "that she wanted to spend more time with 'the apostles' teaching . . . the breaking of bread and the prayers'" (quoting Acts 2:42).

These are all examples of voluntary poverty. It's a spectrum, obviously, not a one-size-fits-all definition. There are also, of course, people like Crete, or like St. Francis of Assisi (who was Peter Maurin's model), who more nearly divest themselves of everything and live by begging for food and shelter.

But it's important, too, to mention those on the other side of the spectrum who, as our tradition sometimes puts it, live in the *spirit* of voluntary poverty. My friends the Johnsons are a case in point. They have a house in the suburbs, send their kids to private schools, and have plenty of expendable income. No one would say they were *poor.* But they take the Gospel seriously and increasingly are finding that their relationship to their wealth is an important aspect of their faith. They've started thinking and talking about how they might move *toward* a simpler life.

These are wonderful, generous people; they make it a point to actively support communities like ours and have made regular contributions not only of cash, but of labor and in-kind donations. They've even organized fundraisers at their parish for us and invited us to come and speak.

And the Johnsons raise a further point that is important to keep in mind as we proceed through this chapter. As in the case of the other "radical" elements of Peter and Dorothy's vision, voluntary poverty is a matter of the little way, and this means it is a matter of the baby steps by which any kind of change takes root in our lives. Sometimes there are big steps along the way—like the day Mallory decided to quit her job—but even that decision only came as one in a series of mostly imperceptible, slow, incremental changes in their lives. Jesus's teaching about wealth is radical, no doubt; but he always meets us where we are, even when he is calling us to something more.

So, as we'll see in more detail below, in spite of the images the phrase might conjure up, for most of us voluntary poverty does not mean dirt, destitution, danger, or living on the street. It means primarily a certain simplicity of life that gives us the freedom to practice the Gospel in a more thoroughgoing way and that binds us together more tightly with our community.

In the rest of this chapter, we'll explore why voluntary poverty is such an important part of the kinds of Catholic communities we've been envisioning.

Jesus on Wealth and Poverty

The first question, though, is why this issue comes up at all. Many Catholics haven't heard of voluntary poverty, and if they have, then only as something monks do. Why would Dorothy and Peter think it has anything to do with you or me?

Before we get to the reasons for it, the first thing to note is just that it's absolutely central to Jesus's own example and teaching. Not only does he tell us that it's our job to care for the poor personally, as we've seen, but he also clearly calls his followers to embrace some measure of poverty themselves—it is undeniably a key theme.

Just take a look at some of these texts:

- "Blessed are you poor," he says, "for yours is the kingdom of God" (Lk 6:20).
- "Whoever of you does not renounce all that he has cannot be my disciple" (Lk 14:33).
- Accordingly, "Behold," says Peter, "we have left everything and followed you" (Mt 19:27).
- "'If you would be perfect,'" he tells a rich young man, "'go, sell what you possess and give to the poor . . . and come, follow me.' When the young man heard this he went away sorrowful; for he had great possessions" (Mt 19:21–22).
- "Do not lay up for yourselves treasures on earth . . . but lay up for yourselves treasures in heaven. . . . For where your treasure is, there will your heart be also" (Mt 6:19–21).
- "Consider the ravens: they neither sow nor reap; they have neither storehouse nor barn, and yet God feeds them. Of how much more value are you than the birds!" (Lk 12:24).
- "Give to him who begs from you, and do not refuse him who would borrow from you" (Mt 5:42).

- He tells a parable that implies that if you do not forgive debts others owe you, God won't forgive your sins (see Matthew 18:21–35).
- He tells a story about a rich man who was sent to hell, apparently just for being rich, and a poor man who went to heaven, apparently just for being poor (see Luke 16:19–31).
- On the other hand, he doesn't mince words about the danger of riches: "Woe to you that are rich, for you have received your consolation" (Lk 6:24).
- Jesus tells a parable about a man who built a barn for himself to store all his excess goods: "God said to him, 'Fool! This night your soul is required of you'" (Lk 12:20).
- "Truly, I say to you, it will be hard for a rich man to enter the kingdom of heaven. Again I tell you, it is easier for a camel to go through the eye of a needle than for a rich man to enter the kingdom of God" (Mt 19:23–24).

Jesus himself was voluntarily homeless during his ministry—he had "nowhere to lay his head" (Lk 9:58). Because he was homeless, it made sense for him to say to his disciples that whatever you do to the poor, the homeless, the sick, or the imprisoned, "you did to *me*" (Mt 25:40): he literally was a poor, homeless man. *This* is the Jesus whom we're supposed to follow, and that's what Tony, the Cross family, and Mallory were up to: trying to put this aspect of the Gospel into practice.

The reason that voluntary poverty comes up in this book about Christian community is simply that it's all over the gospels, and so it wouldn't be *Christian* community without it.

Why, more specifically, is this discipline so important?

Poverty and Freedom

Far and away the most cited reason for voluntary poverty in the Catholic tradition is that it allows us to be *detached* from things in order to be *attached* to God. In other words, it gives us interior freedom.

We usually want money because with it we think we can control our lives. But too often our money ends up controlling us. Possessions may make our lives more comfortable, but too much of the time we end up possessed by *them*. This can make it difficult to serve God, because we are so busy serving and protecting our stuff. And the tricky thing is that so often this can happen without our ever being aware of it.

It is true enough, as is often said, that the issue is not with wealth *itself*. Being rich doesn't automatically make you evil, and being poor doesn't automatically make you a saint.

Having said this, however, we immediately have to be very careful. For far too much of the time, we jump from "riches are not evil" right to "wealth poses no danger for me." We fool ourselves into thinking that we are not attached to our possessions, when most of us really are. In fact, as the Church has long recognized, the reason Jesus is so radical in his words about possessions is that if you have them, it is close to impossible *not* to be attached to them. Hence his counsel is to have as little as possible.

To be *detached* from something is to have no trouble giving it up—it wouldn't faze you if it went away. And so a good barometer of our attachment to our things is if we would be willing to give them up. As a thought experiment, we can ask ourselves if we would be willing not to take out insurance policies on them. Would we be okay if this or that just went away? Usually not, and that is why we spend *extra* money trying to keep them. I am not necessarily suggesting we get rid of all insurance policies, but they are useful in helping us see the condition of our attachments.

Material poverty of some kind, then, is essential to the internal freedom that Christ wants to give us. He wants us to be, as Peter Maurin said, "as free as birds."[1] This is the goal. But Dorothy knew that "those who have only interior poverty, run the risk of having none at all."[2]

How Much?

As we saw in the opening examples, there is no one, uniform standard of wealth applicable to everyone. Exactly how much each of us should have will vary with our circumstances. But the Church does say, and has always said, that no Christian (including the laity) should have more than she needs to sustain her bodily necessities according to her station in life. That is a pretty radical teaching, but it's right there in St. Thomas Aquinas, and, at least implicitly, in the *Catechism*.[3]

What exactly our station in life requires is the part that will vary. There is room for discernment here that can easily be used as a loophole to soften the blow of the Gospel, so perhaps it is clearer to just say, with St. Basil, that our surplus goods belong to the poor.[4] What this means for each person is complex and must be worked out with our own communities and spiritual directors. But what is not complex is that, regardless of our situation, most of us surpass what we really need by a long shot.

This teaching seems so radical to us in part because our culture hands us a preformed vision of what the "good life" is that includes having much more than we will ever use. We are all encouraged to seek a comfortable life with lots of spending money, travel, expensive schools, fancy meals, and the latest tech toys and entertainment. This even becomes part of what being a good, respectable citizen means. From an early age we are indoc-trinated to become the kinds of people who can achieve this kind of life—to be industrious, hardworking, educated, sober, prudent, cautious, self-made, and protective of our money.

We are trained in all kinds of ways to become the kind of people who are *attached* to our wealth, which makes it very hard to hear Jesus's counsel that we be *detached* from it. Jesus tells us that we should not even worry about tomorrow, yet most of us grew up learning that to be a responsible adult is to spend most of our time doing exactly that.

Poverty and Community

But the most pressing reason for voluntary poverty today, and the one most germane to this book, is that voluntary poverty in the Catholic sense both requires and creates community. I'll say how in a minute, but we can note right away that this means that Jesus didn't ever intend his admittedly radical words about wealth and possessions to be practiced by individuals in isola-tion. I think one of the main reasons we so easily dismiss them as impractical is that we imagine we'd have to do them all by ourselves. We assume we'd continue to live our familiar atom-ized, anxious, virtual, fragmented existence, only without any money or resources. Sounds fun, right?

But this is not what Dorothy and Peter thought Jesus had in mind at all. He addresses his radical words *to the Church,* to *groups* of disciples who would live them out *together.* This is the explicit audience, for instance, of the Sermon on the Mount (see Matthew 5:1). Jesus is giving us a communal ethic, not one that we are to follow in the privacy of our own homes. And when we get this straight, it becomes clear that voluntary poverty is in fact an essential foundation for building the Acts 2 Church.

That's the Church, after all, that the same disciples who heard the Sermon on the Mount would eventually become a part of.

We saw this firsthand—again, mostly by accident—in Durham. This was not least because most of us were, for various reasons, already fairly poor. Many of us were students, and few of us had yet, as they say, "established ourselves." So, reading Christ's words about money, we made a virtue out of a necessity. Like most of our story, voluntary poverty was a matter of becoming intentional about the gifts that God had already surrounded us with, even before we knew they were gifts.

The basic dynamic is very simple—almost common sense: voluntary poverty in community consists in sharing both wealth and expenses with others. This means you can live on much less—you can simplify your life—and at the same time you create a community that is cohesive because its members all need one another.

The Maurin House's finances were pretty simple. We had half a dozen donors or so who contributed about $100 a month each. About five of us rent-paying residents each chipped in about $200 a month. That mostly took care of rent and utilities. Most of our donors were close friends, and their help bound us even more closely with them. Friends like the Johnsons, mentioned above, who found some extra cash to support us, were essential here. They were part of the house even though they didn't live with us, because we couldn't do it without them. They were, in a way, participating in our voluntary poverty—even making it possible.

Probably about a quarter of the food in our refrigerator at any given time came from in-kind donations and dumpster diving. There was breakfast at St. Joe's five days a week, of course, too, which the ladies from the Presbyterian church donated. At most house dinners, which we had three nights a week, guests from the community would bring a dish to share. This meant that on any given day a significant percentage of what we had eaten came as a gift.

For the rest of our food, we had a fairly unstructured system. People contributed what they could, when they could: a few bags of groceries here, a trip to KFC before Monday night house dinner there. This was as likely to come from the Guys as from the rest of us. We intentionally left it unformalized like this in order to stress the point of personal responsibility and attentiveness to one another.

We also shared vehicles. For a few years I had gotten by without owning a car, but there were often errands or commitments that required one. Probably about half of us living in the house had a car, however, and so it was usually convenient to borrow one. The rest of the time most of us walked, biked, or took the bus. If there was a day when all the vehicles were being used and someone had to get somewhere, with a little creative rearranging or carpooling we were usually able to accommodate everyone. Living in community, lack becomes an opportunity for cooperation and for the recognition that our possessions are not just our own but are to be used for the common good.

And then we shared all kinds of little things as well: books, washing machines, garden tools, luggage, vacuum cleaners—you name it. The point, of course, wasn't to save money, but we ended up doing that as well. It just cost much less to live in community than alone. During that time I lived on about $27,000 a year that I made at my half-time church job. And this, it turned out, was *much* more than enough. Looking back, I'm a little embarrassed at the amount I spent at local restaurants on food and beer— usually three or four times a week. But despite this extravagance, there was still plenty in the bank.

Once again, the principle at work is that a community is strengthened when its members are materially or financially dependent upon one another. Sharing wealth acts like a gravitational force that attracts real social ties, much like the way labor functioned in our analysis of preindustrial society. In other words, it's another aspect of reimagining life in terms of the projects we talked about back in chapter 3. When we need one another, material life begins to be taken up into the common good—we start to consider what we do with our stuff in light of how it contributes to others' welfare.

Usually, of course, in our society, things work in the opposite direction. We avoid material dependence on our friends because we are afraid that we will inconvenience them, or they us. We choose, instead, dependence on large impersonal institutions and corporations that we count on to supply us with all the commodities and services that make our fragmented lives possible. We are no longer members primarily of local communities, churches, neighborhoods, and so on, but of Target, Amazon, Allied Health Care, and State Farm. In the process, we become ever more dependent upon our jobs and spend our lives in the constant fear of losing them.

The Gospel Is Risky

But perhaps the most life-changing thing we came to share in Durham was *risk*. Part of the point of voluntary poverty is that it creates a certain amount of precarity that is *good* for us. It's an intentional way of putting our trust in the Lord. For, in spite of our culture's obsession with being prudent in finances (an obsession that often bleeds over into the Church), there is in Jesus's life and teaching undeniably a strong element of throwing caution to the wind for the sake of the Gospel and trusting the Lord to take care of physical necessities. It's the pagans, Jesus says, who worry about having food, shelter, and clothing. Yet we are to "seek first [God's] kingdom," and "all these things shall be yours as well" (Mt 6:31–33).

Jesus, we might even say, invites us to *dare* him to show up and provide for us. He wants us to risk it all for him. And the point, I think, in passage after passage of scripture, is for us to relinquish enough material control over our lives that we can *see* God taking care of us. When *we* provide everything for ourselves, what is there to have faith in?

There's an old legend that the Jewish rabbis tell in this regard. When the Jews were coming out of Egypt and on the edge of the Red Sea, God had told them he was going to part the waters, but no one would take the first step in. So finally an old man put his toe in the water. Nothing. He went in up to his knees. Nothing. To his waist. Still nothing. All the way up to his neck. Still the people watched and waited. Finally he took another step and allowed the water to go up over his nose and eyes and *right then* the waters parted.

Faith involves real risk—including real financial risk. If there's no chance of loss in your Christianity, you might be reading a different New Testament than I am. But, paradoxically, the Gospel also transforms the very nature of risk, so that it is no longer something we have to spend our whole lives avoiding.

In Durham there was a handful of us living well under the poverty line together in one household. There was always a fair chance that, through loss of job or unexpected expenses, one of us was going to be broke every once in a while. But we became, as it were, one another's insurance policy. In other words, we all had the other guy's back, materially and financially.

Because none of us needed very much, there was always enough to go around. And because everyone knew they might have to inconvenience others, no one was inconvenienced when someone needed help. We learned from the poor that those who have little do not assume that money is a private affair, and they are not embarrassed or judgmental when someone is not able to take care of all their own expenses.

"Being short," as they say, is just part of life, and it happens often. It's part of what community *is* to supply our neighbor's lack. Ironically it's often those who have plenty to give who act as if it only belongs to them, and, as a result, they usually feel isolated and alone.

But it was not just inside the community that we could rely upon others. We discovered that because we were invested in the local neighborhood, and the local diocese as well, we had a growing number of friends, like the Johnsons, who supported the spirit of what we were up to, even if they couldn't fully join us themselves. At one point I counted as many as fifty people in the city whom I knew I would always be able to turn to in a pinch for rent money, a couch to sleep on, or even a quiet house and yard to take a retreat at every once in a while (as I often did).

In all of this, I discovered a new kind of security. In the spirit of the little way, we were taking baby steps toward reestablishing community founded on friendship and shared commitments to the Gospel, rather than on shoring up our own private financial futures. The world seemed to open up and became much less scary.

As I said at the outset, all of this can only unfold in baby steps. Today our Catholic Worker community has households of children as well as of the poor. As seen with the Cross family, voluntary poverty is in some ways easier for those of us with families and in some ways harder than it was for us when we were single. We have to continue to be intentional about making financial decisions that build our lives together rather than apart. Sharing a mortgage, not keeping track of who "owes" whom for what, coordinating two cars between families (rather than, say, four), and having a common backyard and garden are all ways we try to blur the lines between "mine" and "thine." We have to constantly remind one another that learning to be friends today means learning to inconvenience one another.

Conclusion

Peter and Dorothy advocated voluntary poverty not just as a radical devotional practice for individuals but as a key to combating the radical individualism of the age. This kind of simplicity is the determination to substitute friendship for insurance, community for savings accounts, divine providence for risk management.

But all this is also, most profoundly, a way that we are invited to a greater intimacy with Christ himself. For poverty is not just something incidental to Christ's life, as if he just happened to be poor because he lived at a time when most people were poor. His poverty, rather, is an essential part of who he *is*—his poverty is not only an aspect of his mission to save us, but part of his revelation of the very nature of God.

For poverty is part of the whole mystery of redemption in which Christ "emptied himself, taking the form of a servant" (Phil 2:7). Poverty is part of this "emptying"; like his Passion and Cross, his poverty was also for our sake (see 2 Corinthians 8:9). And so, like all of Christ's life, poverty reveals to us something essential about God himself.

Just like any aspect of the pursuit of holiness, then, voluntary poverty is part of becoming more Christlike—it is a way to deepen our relationship with him, to experience more of his life as our life, to draw closer to him in order to "become partakers of the divine nature" (2 Pet 1:4). Knowing poverty is an essential part of knowing God.

And the genius of the Catholic Worker is to recognize that living voluntary poverty is not something we ever do alone, but something we do as a community whose bonds are the Gospel.

Each of those bonds is, as it were, a little piece of Christ himself: his prayer, his meals with us, his presence in the poor, his work with his own hands, and, finally, his own poverty. The point of the Church is that it embodies these various parts of him in real life, so *as the Church's social fabric* he once again takes flesh for the world. This is what it means that the Church is his *body*. And this is why poverty is an essential element of the Christian life, for there is no other way that the world can see Jesus.

CONCLUSION: A FORETASTE OF THE KINGDOM

My friend Tyler, who now helps run the hospitality house we have in Minneapolis, often describes his first experience of coming to the Maurin House back in Durham: "My wife and I went to evening prayer one night and were invited back to the house afterward for community dinner," he says. "And there we found the strangest assortment of people you could imagine. Here were graduate students, neighbors, homeless people, black, white, rich, poor, gay, straight, Christians, a Jew, agnostics.

"Bubba is chatting up the neighbors.

"Crete is standing in the kitchen over a pot of beans telling a student that his pants make him look like Michael Jackson, which is meant to be a compliment, but the student isn't so sure.

"Danny is on the front porch smoking and telling Charlie about his time in Vietnam.

"Old Mac is complaining to Young Mac that Crete is picking all the meat out of the soup.

"That was not a kind of party I had ever been to before," Tyler says, "but I knew I had to come back."

What Ty describes is a common miracle. It's common because it's certainly not limited to that community. But it's a

miracle because what he describes is nothing less than a foretaste
of the kingdom of God. And this is what the Church and the
Catholic Worker are all about.

The chapters of this book have tried to sketch briefly a vision
of what the Church can be, and what it will have to be, moving
into the future. We've said it often enough: small communities
of liturgy, friendship with the poor, food, celebration, hospitality, voluntary poverty, sacramental life, all made up of robustly
Catholic, little way, dirt-loving demon fighters.

The Church as Foretaste

But these words are just a long-winded way of saying what Tyler
experienced that night, right in front of his face. It was an experience of the *kingdom of God.*

We all know that Christ has promised to return at the end
of time to set all things right and to establish his kingdom. For
Catholics, this doesn't mean being whisked off to some oth-
er-worldly realm of chubby angels singing on clouds. Rather, in
scripture, "heaven" is most often pictured as a *renewed earth* (see
Isaiah 65:17, 66:22). This, presumably, includes a redeemed and
renewed society: redeemed work, renewed but real relationships,
human community, and many other aspects of life we have now,
just transfigured and brought to perfection.

This kingdom will be "earthy" enough that the prophet Isaiah
can describe it this way:

> The wolf shall dwell with the lamb,
>   and the leopard shall lie down with the kid,
> and the calf and the lion and the fatling together,
>   and a little child shall lead them.
> The cow and the bear shall feed;
>   their young shall lie down together;

and the lion shall eat straw like the ox.
The sucking child shall play over the hole of the asp,
    and the weaned child shall put his hand on the
        adder's den.
They shall not hurt or destroy
    in all my holy mountain;
for the earth shall be full of the knowledge of the Lord
    as the waters cover the sea. (Is 11:6–9)

And the crazy claim of the Church, a claim made especially often by the early Church, is that it exists now precisely as a *foretaste* of that peaceable kingdom that is to come.

In that kingdom, the center of everything will be the constant corporate worship of Christ in the flesh. This is why the center of the Church today is the worship of Christ's Body and Blood in the Mass.

In that kingdom, all of space and time will be taken up into that worship. That is why we sanctify all our days with the corporate common prayer of the Liturgy of the Hours.

In that kingdom, we will rediscover our relationship not only with God but also with our brothers and sisters. Our alienation from one another will end, and we will fully realize the truth that we always only *are* as parts of one another. That is why we celebrate, whenever we can, the simple joy of being together.

In that kingdom, the last will be first and the first will be last. At the last trumpet, says one writer, right behind Christ and the saints will come the innumerable army of the poor, gathered from throughout history.[1] We make our lives with them now, simply as poor, because they are the first citizens of the kingdom. That is why we lavish our goods upon them and seek to become poor ourselves.

In that kingdom, "creation itself will be set free from its bondage" (Rom 8:21), and our physical bodies will not be cast off, but renewed. There, not in disembodied bliss, but on a new

earth (see Revelation 21:1), we will once again realize our vocation as stewards of that earth. That is why we now seek good
work, why we seek to get close to the soil, why we shorten the
supply chains.

The Church, then, is what it is and does what it does because
it is a foretaste of the kingdom. Every time some element of it
is realized—at Mass, at Tyler's party, or at your weekly Bible
study—that is the future that has become a reality. Or rather,
it's the way the eternal realm of God and the saints reaches into
our here-and-now realm, however partially and brokenly. It's the
kingdom that has come on earth as it is in heaven.

Behind Enemy Lines

This vision of the Church as pockets of the kingdom of God
fits with the reality that today we practice our faith not as part
of a dominant Christian culture, but as foreigners in a strange
land. We live at a time when we can't just coast; we have to be
intentionally faithful every day. Christianity is an ongoing battle.

For this we may be thankful, for it constantly reminds us
that, as we have seen, this war is not merely spiritual, internal,
and invisible. It's going on materially and socially right in front
of our eyes. The world is still God's good creation, but it has, very
obviously, been occupied by rebellious forces. We live behind
enemy lines.

Into this occupied territory God has sent his Church. In
his wisdom, this is his way of winning the war. But also, in his
wisdom, the Church's mission does not obey the logic of conventional warfare. Its primary mode is not to slowly take back
enemy territory geographically, or even on a broad sociopolit-
ical level, in order to establish itself as the dominant force. The
Church behind enemy lines does not try to *establish* the kingdom

once and for all, here and now, by securing itself in a position of power by political hegemony, legislation, or institutional dominance, much less by conventional warfare.

Rather, the way God has chosen to win back his rebellious world is to plant in it little pockets of people faithful to him. These (usually small) communities are outposts of *his* kingdom, and their people are loyal to Christ the King even while living under the foreign rule of "the god of this world" (2 Cor 4:4). Loyalty means, of course, living by his kingdom's laws and way of life, building its culture, even in the midst of a kingdom and communities hostile to it.

A Precarious Kingdom

This difference between trying to *establish* the kingdom by conventional institutionalization and allowing it to break in by simply practicing the Gospel is important. It's hard to exaggerate the hold that the drive to secure, insure, officially establish, and create new institutions has on us. We like things official. If it doesn't have a legal status, a board, and a website, it doesn't exist.

And so we try to *establish* the kingdom by making it part of the establishment. We make a five-, ten- or twenty-year Church strategy, always angling for the upper hand in something—a greater share of market or property or people or money—which so often has the effect of putting off the actual practice of the Gospel until we secure the space to guarantee that we can practice it safely.

The Church as a foretaste of the kingdom, on the other hand, gets on with simply *living* the kingdom and leaves the future to God, knowing that whatever kind of world ends up coming into being, it will always be possible to live the kingdom in it. The means of this kingdom are always the same as its end. To build it is to perform the same actions as to live it. It always stands waiting to appear right now. That's the miracle Tyler saw.

All this means that the Church's existence will often be precarious. But this must be so, because so was her Lord's. Christ came into his own world, but his world "knew him not" (Jn 1:10). Christ definitively rejected the ways of power, violence, and conventional politics to win back his rebellious world. That's what the temptation scenes between Jesus and the devil are all about (see Matthew 4:1–11). He chose to put down the sword and take up the Cross and to create small communities called to carry that same cross (see Matthew 16:24)—to live the same precarious existence behind enemy lines as a foretaste of the kingdom. He refused the big way and chose the little way.

But, paradoxically, this precarity is precisely what allows us to live with true confidence in the future. For it is only if we were trying to hold on to something for ourselves would we have reason to fear. But we do not fear, for we do not have an interest in shoring up either a conservative or a liberal political or social establishment. For the kingdom doesn't have a social and political platform—it *is* a social and political reality. It's a *kingdom*, after all. When Tyler first attended a community dinner, he had stepped into a different realm, and it ultimately demanded his loyalty.

And because it's a *kingdom*, it takes material and social form. Precarity does not mean that there is no place for Catholic institutions, cooperatives, and formalized patterns of life. It's not to say that there can be no planning or order to life. It's not to deny that life has to take on stable rhythms, that we have to raise children, make money, and care for the weak.

Homeschool co-ops, Christian credit unions, CSAs, educational centers, trade unions, citizens, movements, neighborhood organizations, natural food stores, small businesses, and indeed agronomic universities and hospitality houses themselves are kinds of Catholic institutions that invariably tend to grow out of the movement from cult to culture to cultivation.

But what so often happens is that an institution arising out of the bonds of the Gospel becomes an end in itself and frustrates the very Gospel ends it was created to serve. Then we have a Church run by institutional commitments rather than institutions serving the Gospel. We have a Gospel domesticated by worries about tomorrow when the Gospel itself says not to worry about tomorrow at all (see Matthew 6:34). And so in our rush to secure for the Church a place in the world tomorrow, we sacrifice even having a Church today. And then we don't have one tomorrow either.

Our business is not to secure or establish the Church in this world. That is God's business. Our business is to train our eyes and ears on Christ, his Church, and his practices—to live in and by those and to remain entirely openhanded about any "success" we have. We cannot try to guarantee it will endure. The only way we can prepare its future is to embody it in the present. The weapons that truly defend the Church are not swords and guns, but voluntary poverty, prayer, community, celebration, and the rest.

And the paradox is that wherever the Church *has* tried to establish herself, she has often fallen into decay and become a merely formal institution. But when she has not insisted on establishing herself—when she has focused on faithfulness and let the chips fall where they may—she has usually become vital and strong. "The blood of the martyrs," the Church father Tertullian famously wrote, "is the seed of the Church."[2]

Forgiveness

To be sure, community life can be so hard. This is one of the reasons we reach for formal structures in the first place—and risk community becoming nothing *but* those structures. Community is, I can attest from personal experience, often full of conflict and tensions. People do not naturally get along; we hurt one another; sin is real. It's not easy to live together, as anyone who has ever been married, or even just grown up in a family, can attest.

All of this is even more true of the kinds of Catholic communities Dorothy and Peter founded. At the Maurin House that night when Tyler first visited, there were probably at least two small arguments, one heated one, and lots of little awkward moments. Not only was Mac complaining about Crete picking out the meat, but Danny approached me to complain about Mac, and one guy obviously had too much to drink.

And it wasn't just the homeless Guys. It was the committed Catholic Workers too: Gary had been being passive-aggressive with Mike for the last two weeks because he hadn't been coming to prayer regularly. And Matt was mad at me and thinking of moving out because he didn't like our house dog, who growled at him, and I had not been willing to get rid of the dog. So I thought Matt was being a baby.

Anyone who expects real Christian community to be heart-to-hearts and kumbaya around the campfire has never experienced it. Conflict is the *normal* state of things.

And that's just the point. Part of the purpose, in God's wisdom, of the Church as *community* is to show us our faults and failings. It's easy to imagine, when we keep to ourselves, that we've got it all together. "I don't commit crimes, and I'm not an alcoholic, and I don't usually have mortal sins to confess, and in general I tend to get along with people." But this is a pretty limited set of criteria for ourselves. Community exposes our selfishness, greed, lust for power, fear, control issues, and all the rest. It leaves us fewer illusions about what we, our friends, or the average person on the street is really like.

And this is why the Church must always be a community of *forgiveness*. We need sacramental Confession certainly, but also mutual, one-on-one, face-to-face conversations of "I'm sorry I did that; please forgive me" and "I forgive you." This is perhaps the most important way that the Church is a foretaste of the kingdom. When Christ establishes his kingdom, we will all be there as forgiven sinners. None of us will deserve to be there, and, though there will be degrees of holiness, no one will think of oneself as "better" than another. For we will all be there only because we have been continually forgiven by God and by one another.

This is why confession and forgiveness, both sacramental and interpersonal, is utterly essential to the Church. If the Church is life in community, it is also life as forgiveness. Community gives us much more matter for the confessional, that is for sure, and we should make frequent use of it. But community also forces me to become the kind of person who both asks for and gives forgiveness regularly to my brothers and sisters. God wants to make us forgiven forgivers: that is why he gave us one another.

Far from making community sullen or depressing, practicing forgiveness in fact is a source of freedom and joy. For it is a constant invitation to take ourselves less seriously than we usually do. The angels can fly, G. K. Chesterton wrote somewhere, only because they take themselves so lightly. This is the true humility that stands at the heart of Christian spirituality, and we can only get it by being forgiven and forgiving "seventy times seven" times (Mt 18:22).

For we simply *are* going to sin against one another, and often. On the one hand, this is not something to celebrate, and we should use the call to community as an invitation to fight against these sins. But on the other hand, it's a truth we can embrace about ourselves with a certain sense of humor, because God has not seen our sin as more significant than his grace. He takes us lightly because his mercy far exceeds our denial of it.

In his Sacred Heart, Jesus has not just given the possibility for personal reconciliation with God but also provided for the possibility of a kind of community the world does not know. A community of mutual confession and forgiveness is a community that need not be destroyed by its many sins, tensions, and conflicts. A party like what Tyler described should not be possible in this world, but it is, because the kingdom is real, and we have a foretaste of it right now.

Idealistic and Utopian

The Church's job, then, is simply to be the social and material embodiment of that future kingdom in this fallen world.

We are this embodiment very imperfectly. We are only, to be sure, a poor reflection of that perfect society we one day hope to experience. But the point is that we are simply called to be that reflection. We are a communal gesture toward that reality, and without the whole Gospel, the gesture doesn't make sense. We are not at liberty to domesticate it, or to trim off the parts of it that are especially difficult and make something "more sustainable" here below.

This means we will likely look foolish in our efforts, because we will fail so often. But our very holy-foolery—our willingness to let our best efforts be enough, and for our sufficiency to rest in the Lord alone—is *part of* the kingdom. By our very attempts, God wants to hold out to the world a glimpse of what redeemed community, and indeed redeemed humanity, can look like and will one day become.

Catholicism, then, is implacably and unapologetically ideal-istic. We do not settle for what is prudent or feasible in the eyes of the world, or even what we can realistically expect ourselves to ever become here below. The Church's vocation is to be a fore-taste. We are the servants of that ideal. We *have* to be idealistic.

Too often the Church has found this vocation hard and given up on it. We see that it doesn't "work" or "fit" with this world. Therefore, it is always only partially realized, it always limps, and it often appears and then disappears too quickly. So we have called it utopian and settled for mediocrity. We have ridiculed the idealistic, institutionalized sanctity, exalted prudence, and created a lowest-common-denominator Christianity that shames us for having any aspirations beyond middle-class, well-insured religiosity.

We have not realized that in limiting the Gospel to what seems possible in this world we have betrayed it, precisely because the Gospel is not possible on this world's terms. We have tried to have Christianity on this world's terms and won-dered why the Gospel doesn't work. But the whole point of living behind enemy lines is that the Gospel is a way of life designed for *another* world. We are right that it doesn't fit or work and that it is hard. But that doesn't make it any less the Gospel. Again, our vocation is to be a foretaste.

So the critics are right: the Gospel *is* utopian. "Utopia" literal-ly means a "no-place." And that, in a certain way, is exactly what the Church is. It's a politics that finds no place in the current world. It's a social reality that does not make sense, and does not fit, within the confines of the present, because it is the breaking into this present world of the world that is to come. If we are not utopians, then we are just the present world.

Yet the world to come is the one that this world, including us, is made for. The Church reveals the deepest reality, the *true* laws, of creation: the way things are designed to work, but that are now shrouded in darkness and sin. The Gospel reveals, you might say, the grain of the universe and calls us to live with that grain and not against it. In other words, it is not that the Gospel is unrealistic; it is that the ways of the world are not realistic enough. If we want to be really reasonable, sensible, and realistic, then we must be Catholic utopians.

The Beauty of the Kingdom

My hope for this little book is that it might convey a little of the beauty that captured me at St. Joe's and that hooked Tyler. For at the end of the day, I am convinced that beauty is what Dorothy and Peter's vision for the Church today is really about: a challenge to recover a properly Catholic "aesthetic." The Church is God's artwork, and when people gaze upon it, they should see the heart of the Artisan. It should dramatize the life of Jesus Christ in all its grit, fellowship, sacrifice, humor, and joy.

When people think of the Church today, they should imagine something like what Tyler and I saw. This is the beauty that is proper to the Church, not as a human institution or as something that we can make, but as the kingdom breaking in among us.

For the Lord has chosen this beauty to be the way that his kingdom is present now, even in this world devastated by the Enemy. And this kingdom takes root and spreads precisely because its beauty is compelling. Simply to perceive it is already to be drawn into it. From there we must either reject it by running away or accept it by going in deeper. Either way we will have to change our life. The beauty of the kingdom forces a decision.

The Church goes forward in the world, then, not by reasoned argument, not by political power, not by relevant programs or savvy advertising, and not by finding a place in the establishment, but because it makes a space for a compelling beauty, which is ultimately Jesus Christ himself. It is this beauty that draws the world to the Church and draws all of us deeper into its intoxicating mystery.

"The world," Dorothy used to quote Dostoyevsky, "will be saved by beauty." That beauty is the kingdom of God, and that is what the Church must hold out to the world.

On the one hand, it is not something that can be engineered; it comes about only as a gift. We cannot create it; it is not something that *we* can give. It is only something we can make way for. It can only precariously occur.

On the other hand, paradoxically, the kingdom only arrives as a visible, social form. Christ's beauty always has to be materialized in our midst. It can only occur if we *actually live* the Gospel. There is no shortcut, no way to create it online, no way to fake it, no way to produce an insured version of it that would guarantee that we can produce it without anyone losing their money or their reputation or their life. Paradoxically, the beauty of the kingdom is pure gift, but it only comes if we practice it.

And this is usually the sticking point. We are so used to a Church that has tried to have Christianity while minimizing the extent to which anyone has to actually *act* like a Christian that we are not sure how we could ever get started.

And so we just have to start. Taking Dorothy and Peter, the scriptures, and the lives of the saints as our guides, we just have to be brave and take a first step. Figuring out what exactly this means is up to each of us, in our own families, in our own communities.

Say prayers as a family. Or invite your neighbors to a potluck. Go to work through the poor part of town. Find out where to buy local food. Establish a monthly meal with people from your parish. Sell one of your cars and carpool with your spouse. Take the bus. Talk to the guy holding the sign; give him money. Plant a garden. Or visit a homeless encampment. Each one of these things *is* the little way of fighting the demons, *is* building a new society within the shell of the old, *is* the beauty of the kingdom, right now.

It will be natural to feel that, at each step, you want someone to tell you what to do next. And to some extent, there is guidance to be found. There are other books you can read; you can pick the brains of local Catholic Workers; you can join another intentional community in your area. You can talk to your pastor or spiritual director. These are all wise things to do, and you should always seek counsel from trusted friends.

Ultimately, however, it's your life, and no one is going to tell you how to live it. You are not going to receive a call from your priest outlining a plan. That's not his job, and he couldn't tell each of his parishioners how they should live the Gospel in each of their lives if he wanted to. It's our job, each of us, as Catholics, to take the Gospel seriously and to courageously step out and blaze new trails. You are going to have to *act*, not knowing what the results will be.

One of the most remarkable things about the early Church was that they did exactly this. They knew *what* they had to do— the Church told them that—but that didn't tell them *how* to do it in their particular situations, and they didn't know what would happen when they did. Neither did Dorothy and Peter. Neither do we.

One thing we can be sure of is that we are probably going to "fail" more often than we "succeed." This was true for the early Church, as well as for Dorothy and Peter. At the same time, we'll have to be very clear that, for us, "success" often looks like "failure," just as it did for the martyrs, and just as it did for our Lord. For all these, to be a Christian was to look profoundly foolish. But then, the wisdom of God *is* foolishness to the world (see 1 Corinthians 1:18).

The days of respectable Christianity are gone. We have to once again get used to looking like fools for Christ. And the miracle is that by being such fools—together—we discover, even now, the joy for which we are destined. That joy—and the broken, precarious, miraculous, beautiful community that gives rise to it—is surely what keeps me a Catholic Worker to this day. That joy, too, is a taste of the kingdom.

NOTES

1. The Gospel as Social Fabric

1. Peter Maurin, "What the Catholic Worker Believes," Catholic Worker, accessed October 9, 2023, https://catholicworker.org/easy-essays-html/#what-the-catholic-worker-believes. This entire Easy Essay will be quoted in a subsequent chapter.

2. Blowing the Dynamite of the Church

1. Peter Maurin, "Blowing the Dynamite," Catholic Worker, accessed October 4, 2023, https://catholicworker.org/easy-essays-html/#blowing-the-dynamite.

4. Dorothy and Peter

1. Peter Maurin, "What the Catholic Worker Believes," *Catholic Worker*, accessed October 9, 2023, https://catholicworker.org/easy-essays-html/#what-the-catholic-worker-believes.

2. Dorothy Day, *The Long Loneliness* (New York: Harper and Row, 1952), 285.

3. See Peter Maurin's Easy Essay "Counsels of the Gospel," in *The Forgotten Radical Peter Maurin: Easy Essays from the Catholic Worker*, ed. Lincoln Rice (New York: Fordham, 2020), 211. This Easy Essay, along with some others, is not included in the online resource I've been citing so far. This edited work by Rice is now the best and most complete collection of Maurin's writings.

5. Celebration

1. Dorothy Day, *The Long Loneliness* (San Francisco: HarperOne, 1996), 285.

2. See *Catechism of the Catholic Church* §1324.

3. J. R. R. Tolkien, *The Two Towers* (London: HarperCollins, 1991), 697.

6. The Poor

1. I am indebted to theologian Samuel Wells for much of what follows in this chapter. Though I have often inflected the themes in my own ways, and adapted them to my own context, I don't think any of the substance is original to me. I internalized most of these ideas in the form of several (as far as I know) yet-unpublished talks he gave around 2010–2012, the text of which he kindly made available to me. Some of this material has also been incorporated into his many books, such as his *Nazareth Manifesto: Being with God* (Malden, MA: Wiley-Blackwell, 2015) and *Incarnational Mission: Being with the World* (Grand Rapids, MI: Eerdmans, 2018). But most of what I learned from Sam wasn't from his books; he was one of my mentors when he was Dean of Duke Chapel, and he was a great support in helping me think through (what he once called) "the Concrete thing."

7. The Little Way

1. Charles E. Moore, "Introduction," in *Called to Community: The Life Jesus Wants for His People*, ed. Charles E. Moore (New York: Plough Publishing, 2016), xv.

2. Maurin would often say this, as Day reports in her May 1974 article, "On Pilgrimage," *Catholic Worker*, accessed January 12, 2024, https://catholicworker.org/540-html/. It is unclear if Maurin himself ever wrote it down.

8. Cult, Culture, and Cultivation

1. Wendell Berry, "The Melancholy of Anatomy," *Harpers Magazine*, February 2015, https://harpers.org/archive/2015/02/the-melancholy-of-anatomy/.

2. See Leo XIII, *Rerum Novarum* §9. We'll take this up in more detail in the next chapter.

3. I don't think this way of reading the text is incompatible with what it says about *God* coming down and actively confusing their languages. The Bible often speaks about God actively doing things that might equally be described as the built-in tendencies of human nature that he has given us. (So, for instance, in Exodus 9:12, God "hardened the heart of Pharaoh," which is just a way of saying the Pharoah rejected God.) The only thing that would be worse than this fragmentation, the Genesis text seems to be saying, is if we had no such tendency that might hinder our quest for alternative unity. In that case, the point appears to be, "Who knows what they might do?"

4. See, for instance, *Rerum Novarum* §3, accessed January 12, 2024, https://www.vatican.va/content/leo-xiii/en/encyclicals/documents/hf_l-xiii_enc_15051891_rerum-novarum.html.

9. A Philosophy of Labor

1. There's a growing cottage industry of Catholic literature, programs, and intentional communities dedicated to reimagining work. See, just for a sample, St. Joseph's Farm (stjosephsfarm.com), New Polity in general (newpolity.com) as well as specific talks such as "Working Class Blues" (July 6, 2023, newpolity.com/podcasts-hub//33u1kl5c9s81q9grdi6beqekb4rjkl), the new College of St. Joseph the Worker (collegeofstjoseph.com), St. Isidore Academy (stisidoreacademy.com), and many more.

2. Leo XIII, *Rerum Novarum* §9; italics added for emphasis.

3. This is a major theme of St. John Paul II's encyclical *Laborem Exercens*.

4. *Rerum Novarum* §§9-10.

5. *Rerum Novarum* §2.

6. *Rerum Novarum* §51. See also, even more forcefully, Pope Pius XI's encyclical *Quadragesimo Anno*, §§25 and 49, and throughout.

7. See *Rerum Novarum* §1, where he introduces the very notion of modern work by talking about how much it has *changed* things.

8. See, for instance, *Rerum Novarum* §§46–48, 55.

10. Gardens, Chickens, and Dumpsters

1. Leo XIII, *Rerum Novarum* §3.

2. *Rerum Novarum* §3.

11. Voluntary Poverty

1. Peter Maurin's Easy Essay, "What St. Francis Desired," *Catholic Worker*, accessed October 4, 2023, https://catholicworker.org/easy-essays-html/#what-saint-francis-desired.

2. Pie-Raymond Regamey, OP, *Poverty: An Essential Element in the Christian Life* (New York: Sheed and Ward, 1949), v. Dorothy Day often recommended this book to others.

3. See St. Thomas Aquinas, *Summa Theologiae* II-II, q. 118, a. 1: "Hence it must needs be that man's good in their respect consists in a certain measure, in other words, that man seeks, according to a certain measure, to have external riches, in so far as they are necessary for him to live in keeping with his condition of life. Wherefore it will be a sin for him to exceed this measure." See *Catechism of the Catholic Church* §2447, quoting St. John the Baptist in Luke 3:11: "He who has two coats, let

him share with him who has none and he who has food must do likewise."

4. St. Basil the Great, "Homily on the saying of the *Gospel according to Luke*, "I will pull down my barns and build bigger ones," §7 (*PG* 31, 277A): "Now, someone who takes a man who is clothed and renders him naked would be termed a robber; but when someone fails to clothe the naked, while he is able to do this, is such a man deserving of any other appellation? The bread which you hold back belongs to the hungry; the coat, which you guard in your locked storage-chests, belongs to the naked; the footwear moldering in your closet belongs to those without shoes. The silver that you keep hidden in a safe place belongs to the one in need. Thus, however many are those whom you could have provided for, so many are those whom you wrong." Translation is from *De Unione Ecclesiarum*, October 8, 2009, https://bekkos.wordpress.com/2009/10/08/st-basil-on-stealing-from-the-poor/.

Conclusion: A Foretaste of the Kingdom

1. I think it was Jacques-Bénigne Bossuet, who is cited often in Pie-Raymond Regamey's *Poverty: An Essential Element in the Christian Life* (New York: Sheed and Ward, 1949). This was also a book Dorothy often recommended, but I have been unable to locate the exact quotation or page number for Bossuet.

2. See Tertullian, *Apology*, 50, accessed January 15, 2024, https://www.newadvent.org/fathers/0301.htm. The literal translation of what Tertullian writes is "The blood of Christians is seed," but this is commonly and rightly taken the way that I have paraphrased it above.

Colin Miller is the director of the Center for Catholic Social Thought at the Church of the Assumption in St. Paul, Minnesota. Miller cofounded a Catholic Worker House in Durham, North Carolina, where he lived and served for several years as a priest in the Episcopal Church. Under the influence of Dorothy Day, Peter Maurin, Augustine of Hippo, John Henry Newman, and many homeless people, Miller was received into the Catholic Church in 2016. After teaching theology for two years, he relocated to Minneapolis where he helped found the Maurin House, a Catholic Worker House devoted to common prayer, material simplicity, and service to the poor.

Miller earned a bachelor of arts degree at the University of Minnesota, a master of arts in religion degree at Yale University, and a PhD from Duke University.

He lives with his family at the Maurin House, a Catholic Worker community in Minneapolis, Minnesota.

Seth Haines is a writer, photographer, and author of *The Book of Waking Up: Experiencing the Divine Love that Reorders a Life* and *Coming Clean: A Story of Faith.*

AVE MARIA PRESS

Founded in 1865, Ave Maria Press,
a ministry of the Congregation of
Holy Cross, is a Catholic publishing
company that serves the spiritual and
formative needs of the Church and its
schools, institutions, and ministers;
Christian individuals and families; and
others seeking spiritual nourishment.

For a complete listing of titles from

Ave Maria Press

Sorin Books

Forest of Peace

Christian Classics

visit www.avemariapress.com

AVE MARIA PRESS
Notre Dame, IN
A Ministry of the United States Province of Holy Cross